D1541728

Investigating Workplace Harassment

Practical HR Series

Investigating Workplace Harassment

How to Be Fair, Thorough, and Legal

Amy Oppenheimer, J.D., and
Craig Pratt, SPHR, MSW
Society for Human Resource Management
Alexandria, Virginia
USA
www.shrm.org

This publication is designed to provide accurate and authoritative information regarding the subject matter covered. It is sold with the understanding that neither the publisher nor the authors are engaged in rendering legal or other professional service. If legal advice or other expert assistance is required, the services of a competent, licensed professional should be sought. The federal and state laws discussed in this book are subject to frequent revision and interpretation by amendments or judicial revisions that may significantly affect employer or employee rights and obligations. Readers are encouraged to seek legal counsel regarding specific policies and practices in their organizations.

This book is published by the Society for Human Resource Management (SHRM). The interpretations, conclusions, and recommendations in this book are those of the authors and do not necessarily represent those of SHRM.

The Society for Human Resource Management (SHRM) is the world's largest association devoted to human resource management. Representing more than 165,000 individual members, the Society's mission is both to serve human resource management professionals and to advance the profession. Visit SHRM Online at www.shrm.org.

Editor: Sharon Lamberton, Editorial Solutions
Indexer: Kate Mertes, Mertes Editorial Services
Cover Designer: Roxanne Walker
Layout: Shirley Raybuck

Library of Congress Cataloging-in-Publication Data

Oppenheimer, Amy, 1952-
    Investigating workplace harassment : how to be fair, thorough, and legal / Amy Oppenheimer, Craig Pratt.
        p. cm. — (Practical HR series)
    Includes bibliographical references and index.
    ISBN 1-58644-030-6
        1. Sexual harassment—Investigation—United States. 2. Sexual harassment—Law and legislation—United States. I. Pratt, Craig, 1948- II. Title. III. Series.
    HF5549.5.S45 O67 2003
    658.3'145—dc21

                                                                        2002004735

Printed in the United States of America.
10 9 8 7 6 5 4 3
                                                                        05-0321

Contents

Examples/Figures

Examples

Figures

Preface

As an attorney representing women who had been sexually harassed at work, I saw everything that went wrong. My clients often were more injured by their employer's lack of response to the harassment than by the harassment itself. Most employers had good intentions—they wanted to do the right thing; they just didn't know how. The cases became a puzzle. What went wrong? How could it have been prevented? This book is my opportunity to provide some of those answers. Avoiding liability is a nice outcome. But my primary goal is to help employers prevent harm.

I was lucky to have the opportunity to train HR investigators with Stephen Anderson. Craig Pratt invited me to investigate cases with him and I was immediately impressed with the patience, care, and skill he brought to the task. Craig's deep concern for the truth and the dedication that he brings to his work is inspiring. I am grateful to have had the opportunity to collaborate with him further in writing this book.

As an investigator I listen to people's intimate thoughts and feelings and I feel graced. Investigations work has taught me the complexity of truth as I view facts from varying perspectives. There are rarely "good guys and bad guys" in these cases. I thank all the people I've interviewed over the years for letting me into their lives and for trusting me.

My "day job" is as an administrative law judge (ALJ) for the California Unemployment Insurance Appeals Board (CUIAB). The work has given me opportunities to determine credibility. CUIAB has allowed me the flexibility to work as an ALJ while pursuing other interests. Our Chief ALJ, Jay Arcellana, and presiding judges Mike DiSanto and Steve Angelides have been particularly supportive and deserve special thanks.

My thanks go to Laura Lawson at SHRM who supported this book from its inception, guided it along the way and graciously answered many questions. Adele Grunberg commented on the manuscript and has been an engaged listener to my musings about various investigations. I am blessed to have a friend with interests so similar to my own.

I am doubly blessed by my family. My beloved, Jennifer Krebs, read the entire manuscript and made valuable suggestions. Perhaps more importantly, she became a single mother to our children countless times while I worked on this book. Thank you Jennifer, Talia, and Adin.

—Amy Oppenheimer

Human resources is my adopted profession and its intricacies have fascinated and engaged me for more than twenty years. Sexual harassment prevention and response became my favorite HR practice area perhaps because I saw in it a chance to act against the injustice I had learned about when, as a child raised by two women, I came to understand the impact of discrimination from those who had experienced it firsthand. Learning to investigate complaints of harassment fairly and with sensitivity has been a consuming passion for me since my earliest investigation experience in 1982. I hope some of the fruit of that passion appears in the pages that follow.

All of us drink water from wells that we have not dug and, to be sure, much of what the reader will find in the pages that follow springs from heartfelt experiences of several people. Witnesses opened their hearts and poured out their stories in scores of investigative interviews. When it was time to write about what I had learned, gifts of rare insight and clear expression flowed from my friend and co-author, Amy Oppenheimer, so many times and places in our work together they are uncountable. Help and encouragement with this first book cascaded from our editor, Laura Lawson. My colleagues, Chris Regan and Bill Kelly, enriched the text with valuable suggestions. My assistant, Lisie Harlow, patiently tended the numerous drafts and revisions. Quietly and with a lack of fanfare my wife Patricia evinced a faith in me that, like an unseen aquifer, sustains all that has gone into creating this work.

—Craig Pratt

Together, we thank Mary Cheddie, Vice President of Human Resources at Orvis, and Douglas B. Mishkin, a Partner in Patton Boggs LLP, both of whom reviewed the manuscript.

Investigating Workplace Harassment

Introduction

Investigating a complaint of workplace harassment can be one of the most challenging tasks for a human resources (HR) professional to undertake. The timely completion of an investigation that has been accurate and fair to all parties is an unmatched professional accomplishment. Investigations require knowledge, patience, and sensitivity. A good investigation—meaning a fair, thorough, and legal investigation—allows an organization to make the right decision as to what action to take. A flawed investigation can lead to countless problems. The importance of a good investigation has increased significantly over the past decade as the law and human resource practice have evolved. Lawsuits for harassment have put investigations under a microscope. When investigations have been found to be adequate, organizations have avoided liability. When investigations have been found to be inadequate, the organization's risk of liability has been significantly greater, as has the risk of larger damage awards.

To complete an adequate investigation of workplace harassment, an investigator must possess certain knowledge and skills. Known techniques can be applied to handle the more difficult parts of an investigation. This book is designed to give you the knowledge you need to investigate a complaint of workplace harassment and to illustrate techniques that will lead to a successful investigation.

This book is designed to provide information on investigating complaints of unlawful workplace harassment. This term means harassment based on an individual's membership in a distinct class, such as harassment based on sex, race, age, religion, disability, and so forth. *Investigating Workplace Harassment* does not cover the investigation of other types of workplace misconduct (such as theft) or complaints of workplace discrimination not involving harassment (such as a discriminatory failure to promote.)

The type of workplace harassment that prompts the most complaints is sexual harassment. Statistics from the Equal Employment Opportunity Commission (EEOC), the federal agency that accepts complaints of discriminatory harassment, show that in the mid-1990s 41% of harassment complaints were based on sexual harassment; 24% based on racial harassment; 21% based on gender-based harassment; 7% based on national origin harassment; and 7% based on other types of unlawful harassment (such as age, religion, and so forth). Statistics from California's Department of Fair Employment and Housing from fiscal year 2000/2001 show that virtually all of the harassment complaints lodged at that agency included an allegation of sexual harassment. Therefore, many of the examples in the book are taken from situations that involved allegations of sexual harassment. The book covers all types of unlawful harassment, however. It also will apply to harassment that is not due to an individual's membership in a distinct class (for example, harassment that takes place simply because an employee is disliked). But that type of harassment usually will not violate laws regarding employment discrimination.

Because all investigations that involve gathering information from employees are similar in many respects, much of the information in this book will be useful for investigating all types of workplace complaints. Some of the information relates specifically to harassment, however. Many skilled investigators who have practiced exclusively in loss prevention or law enforcement lack the necessary skills to handle a harassment complaint. For example, an investigative style that is appropriate to law enforcement cases may be too confrontational to ensure an effective harassment investigation. Do not assume that just because you are an experienced investigator in one area, you have the skills to do an adequate investigation in another area. This book should help you identify which skills you already possess and where you need to increase or polish your skills in order to do a good investigation of harassment.

This book will help you understand the step-by-step nuts and bolts of how to do an investigation. Chapter 1 presents the importance of preparation for a good investigation and discusses some of the challenges an investigation places on an organization and the investigator. Chapter 2 explains the primary laws and legal definitions applicable to workplace harassment while Chapter 3 explains legal matters relating to investigations. Chapter 4 presents information to help you determine when an investigation is necessary, who should investigate, and what the scope of the investigation should be. Chapter 5 covers planning and Chapter 6 addresses documentation. Chapter 7 covers the nuts and bolts of doing the investigation from the start of questioning to the end of the information-gathering phase. Chapter 8 goes into how to assess credibility and evaluate evidence in order to come to a determination. Chapter 9 details what should be contained in a written investigative report and Chapter 10 presents information about remedial actions an organization can take. Chapter 11 deals with training and mediation as techniques to normalize and improve the work environment following an investigation. Appendices provide resources, sample forms, sample statements, and other practical information.

You may use this book two ways. You may follow each step in the order presented or use the materials as a reference to stimulate your thinking and creativity. If you are relatively new to workplace investigations of harassment, we recommend that you read through the entire book and work through all the exercises before you begin an investigation. Each chapter takes you through the steps you need to know. Self-check exercises will help you increase your skills.

If you have training and experience as an investigator of workplace harassment, you may want to use the book as a reference to check your methods and refresh your awareness of various options. For example, if you are wondering how best to document the investigation, you may find the chapter on documentation useful without reading all the chapters in order.

Investigating Workplace Harassment is based on the accumulated experience of the authors, other experts in the field, writings on HR practices, and the law. When the text refers to a legal authority, the reference is stated explicitly and case citations are provided. Many of the examples mentioned are investigations or lawsuits with which one of the authors or a colleague has been involved. These examples illustrate the sorts of situations investigators will contend with but are not legal precedent.

The book may be used alone or as a complement to training. A good training program can be invaluable. It will give you a chance to practice these skills before you have to use them. Experience is a great teacher, and you are encouraged to get as much experience as you can. If you are not ready to investigate on your own, find an experienced investigator with whom you can work. Don't hesitate to ask for help when you need it. If you keep an open mind and an open heart, and if you honestly do your best, you have mastered the most important part of being an investigator.

Preparing for an Investigation of Workplace Harassment

When you begin an investigation you cannot know what the outcome will be. Your ideas about who did or said what to whom may change frequently. Witnesses to the same event may present vastly differing recollections of what happened. Their stories might be irreconcilable. Full of human drama and mystery, investigations are fascinating—and extremely challenging.

How can you prepare yourself for such a task? Doing so may seem like a tall order. An effective investigator must act as a

- detective, uncovering and discovering relevant information from reluctant witnesses;
- therapist, carefully listening without judgment to people's deepest thoughts;
- judge, determining what occurred and ferreting out the truth; and
- reporter, accurately describing what is discovered.

Performing an investigation of workplace harassment will challenge you to practice some of the most sophisticated interpersonal communication skills that you will ever use in your work. To begin, you will need to establish a relationship of trust with two or more individuals who are likely to be distressed. You will have to attempt to maintain that trust while asking difficult, prying questions about matters that many people may find deeply offensive, personal, and embarrassing. Throughout your work you will be trying hard to preserve the rights—including the right to privacy—of the person who complained, the person complained about, and other witnesses.

When you consider all that is necessary to conduct a good investigation, the task can seem daunting. Even after doing everything necessary, you may be unable to say with certainty your conclusion is correct. Nonetheless, the ability to conduct a fair, thorough, and legal investigation of workplace harassment is well within the reach of most human resource practitioners who are proficient in the use of human resources management principles and have experience dealing with employee relations.

Keep in mind that no investigation is perfect. You are not expected to determine the absolute truth; rather, you are expected to be thorough in your quest for the truth and objective in your findings. Most importantly, you are expected to operate *fairly and in good faith*. Investigations that are scrutinized by courts generally are found to be adequate when they have been both thorough and fair.

Prevention and Response

Investigations of harassment are part of an employer's overall prevention and response plan. Prevention of harassment is discussed more thoroughly in Chapter 2. Under the law, employers have a duty not only to respond to complaints of harassment, but also to take all reasonable steps to prevent harassment from occurring. Prevention includes promulgating policies by

- making those policies known to employees through distribution;
- training employees on what harassment is and how to complain about it;
- training supervisors and managers on how to respond to harassment; and
- monitoring the workplace to ensure that no harassment is occurring.

If prevention involves so much effort, why not just wait and respond to actual complaints on a case-by-case basis? The answer is that most people don't complain about harassment. In 1981 the United States Merit Systems Protection Board (MSPB) did a large-scale study of sexual harassment in the federal workplace. The study was updated in 1988 and again in 1995. One clear result was that most victims of harassment did not report the harassment. In the MSPB study, as much as 90% of all harassment incidents went unreported. Figure 1 shows how victims of harassment say they responded. Figure 2 gives the reasons victims gave for not responding.

The fact that most victims don't complain about harassment is why it is so critical that employers take affirmative steps to prevent harassment.

Figure 1. Victims' Responses to Sexual Harassment

Reaction	Males %	Females %
Ignored it	42	52
Asked or told the harasser to stop	25	44
Avoided the harasser	31	43
Made a joke of it	20	20
Reported it to a supervisor	7	15
Threatened to tell or told a peer	8	14
Went along	7	4

Source: A 1988 United States Merit Systems Protection Board (MSPB) study of sexual harassment in the federal workplace

Figure 2. Why Victims Took No Action in Response to Harassment

Reason for No Action	Males %*	Females %*
Had no need to report it	42	44
Thought it would make work situation unpleasant	23	30
Did not think anything could be done	17	23
Did not want to hurt the person who bothered them	20	16
Thought it would be held against me or I'd be blamed	13	17
Too embarrassed	9	14
Did not know what action to take	5	10

*Note: percentages may add up to more than 100 because respondent could indicate more than one response.

Source: A 1988 United States Merit Systems Protection Board (MSPB) study of sexual harassment in the federal workplace

Such affirmative steps include *not* making it mandatory for the victim to tell the perpetrator to stop before complaining about harassment. Many victims are unable or unwilling to do this. Taking affirmative steps also means monitoring the work environment and taking immediate action whenever anything questionable occurs. But even the best prevention plan won't eliminate all harassment from the workplace. When allegations of harassment do arise, the employer must respond—which is where investigations fit in.

Performing a fair and thorough investigation of a harassment complaint is a crucial part of an employer's prevention plan. It commits the organization's resources to backing up its policy and sends the right message to the party who complained as well as everyone else involved in the complaint. It also forms the basis for taking appropriate remedial actions in response to harassment.

Investigating a harassment complaint presents specific challenges to the organization and personal challenges to the investigator. Human resource representatives who conduct investigations often find that the investigative role differs from the other roles they have played in the organization and that some fallout is likely as conflicts emerge among the roles. Before embarking on an investigation it is helpful to think about and anticipate some of these challenges, both for the organization and for yourself.

Challenges for the Organization

Most organizations view harassment complaints as disruptive. Anything that prolongs the discomfort, such as an investigation, is seen as intrusive and potentially harmful. This view of an investigation is perfectly natural but may make the investigation more difficult. The investigator must not only complete a difficult task but also counsel others in the organization on how to properly respond to a sensitive situation. At minimum, an investigator may have to defend the necessity for performing an investigation instead of "letting sleeping dogs lie."

Commitment of Resources

One stress on the organization is that time and resources that normally would be committed to other projects are diverted to the investigation. Some managers may find it hard to accept the need for this. These managers may pressure you to cut corners to complete the investigation quickly and let people "move on." Clearly, closure is important. But first a thorough investigation must take place and such an investigation requires a commitment of resources—sometimes substantial resources—involving departments other than HR. An in-house investigator may have to neglect other work for a week or two, witnesses must be called away from other work, and if an outside investigator is used, the cost and extra disruption of work can be significant.

Organizational leaders, including executives and managers at all levels, play an important role in ensuring a good investigation by providing these resources and respecting the need for an orderly and fair process. Leaders must understand that the extra time (and therefore money) required for the investigation to be as thorough as possible will pay off if the investigation is ever challenged. You may need to enlist help from senior staff in counseling managers to resist the temptation to encourage shortcuts such as telephone interviews with key witnesses.

Potential Conflicts with Managers

The investigator of a harassment complaint needs free rein to call witnesses and review appropriate files and documents. Any interference by a manager with your judgment about what you need to do will compromise the integrity of your investigation. And it is always a mistake for a manager to pressure an investigator for interim reports as to probable investigation findings.

Many managers pride themselves on their ability to handle anything that comes up in their workgroups. Some may conscientiously have attempted to handle conflicts involving the complainant and respondent and therefore, when the complaint is made to HR, they feel betrayed. They fear that they will be seen as ineffective managers—or worse, that HR will now be rummaging around and creating more disruption. They also feel a loss of control because the investigation is out of their hands.

Many executives initially want to deal with a harassment complaint by instructing HR to bring the complainant and the respondent together in a room to "work something out." But doing this would be an unacceptable HR practice in all but the most minor complaints, not least because it would pose significant additional risks to the organization.

HR also needs backing from organizational leaders to make sure that HR (or another specialized unit like Equal Opportunity Employment or Affirmative Action) is notified of every complaint of harassment. If senior staff does not support this approach, there may be inconsistent reporting and inconsistent responses to harassment—and there will be no opportunity for the organization to track harassment complaints. If an alleged harasser receives counseling and then is transferred and repeats the conduct, the harasser's new supervisor will not know about the previous conduct and counseling. This deficiency has serious implications for legal liability. Therefore even managers and supervisors who ordinarily use their discretion to deal with some complaints and report others should be instructed to channel every harassment complaint to HR.

Managers can and should be encouraged to assist the investigation by watching for and reporting any violation of your instructions to witnesses (see Chapter 7) regarding discussions about the investigation interview. Managers should notify you if they observe or suspect that witnesses are talking with each other about the investigation.

How Investigations Affect Employees and Workgroups

Workgroups are likely to be stressed—and distressed—during a harassment investigation and communication frequently is the first casualty. Workgroups may become icily cautious as employees become concerned that they will be reported for any unusual remarks. You can expect increased "rumor mill" activity. Managers must refrain from inadvertently contributing to circulating rumors. Advise managers that the best policy is to refuse to discuss investigation activities and conclusions. If asked, managers should explain that the matter is private and is being handled by the appropriate people.

The circle of employees beyond the complainant and respondent who know about the complaint will inevitably widen as, to achieve a good result, you seek corroboration of the parties' statements from other employees. Some witnesses may use their interviews as an excuse to repeat old stories that reflect poorly on fellow employees, managers, and the organization as a whole. If employees are already split into factions over other issues, some employees may perceive that their adversaries seem to be "winning" because the organization investigates what they consider a spurious complaint. Disgruntled employees may point to the investigation as evidence that they work in a hopelessly substandard unit. All in all, this activity leads to disharmony in the workgroup, a troubling—but often unavoidable—outcome for everyone. As the investigator, you generally will be powerless to do anything about this problem during the investigation. Once the investigation has been completed, you can intervene to help the workgroup come back together (see Chapter 11).

The effects of a harassment complaint on a workgroup will vary based on the culture of the unit. Many workgroups strive for team spirit. Decades of human resources and management training have guided organizations to strive for harmonious workgroups that encourage cooperation and team productivity. Harmony is thought to be easiest to achieve when employees feel good about coming to work and the work atmosphere is informal.

Managers of such workgroups often want to project the image that on their watch "everything is under control" and "our group works as a team." Such a team may see the complainant as someone who is not a team player and mistrust you, the investigator, as an outsider. A complaint of harassment disturbs the informality these types of managers have worked so hard to foster. Complaints of harassment by one or more employees are bitter proof that the unit has failed to achieve harmony. Also, the unfamiliar formality of an investigation can be difficult for these types of workgroups to bear.

Groups in more formal work environments also encounter difficulties. Organizations with a traditional management versus union culture often experience a similar blow to their self-concept, particularly if the complaint is between two represented employees. A problem involving potential harassment of one union member by another may be exacerbated because the union represents the respondent, not the complainant. Thus, the complainant may feel unsupported by his or her own union. Furthermore, most harassment complaints represent a type of conflict that cannot be handled through typical "meet and confer" or grievance procedure processes (Figure 3). Thus, the workgroup finds itself on uncomfortable, strange ground.

A complainant and respondent who belong to the same union may initiate actions against each other according to the union bylaws. Your investigation of the harassment complaint should proceed regardless of such union activity because the employer is responsible for preventing and responding to harassment.

Fast-moving, entrepreneurial workgroups may become very frustrated with HR when it becomes clear how long a thorough investigation will take. The costs in terms of time lost and, in some cases, the fees paid to legal counsel may be particularly difficult for this type of workgroup to accept.

How Investigations Affect Complainants, Respondents, and Witnesses

Complainants, respondents, and, to a lesser extent, witnesses may experience retaliation from the moment a harassment complaint becomes known. Supervisors who had previously overlooked annoying performance deficits may suddenly become assertive about imposing discipline.

Figure 3. Handling Harassment Complaints as Grievances: Not Advisable

Some organizations, especially those with employees represented by unions, look to the structured grievance procedure for handling harassment complaints. The grievance process is a time-tested method for resolving many work disputes, but for several reasons its application to situations involving harassment is problematic. Four primary difficulties come to mind immediately.

1. Harassment allegations rarely depend on an accurate application of contract language because most contract language doesn't cover the types of situations that come up in harassment complaints.

2. The need for privacy and confidential handling of sensitive information is paramount in a harassment complaint. Ordinarily, grievances are automatically forwarded to various parties, including the union's business office. These procedures generally are inflexible and, thus, the appropriate privacy considerations cannot be maintained.

3. The fixed time limits in a typical grievance procedure are unworkable for many harassment complaints and insufficient for investigating allegations.

4. The freedom of a business agent or union steward to negotiate a settlement of a grievance on behalf of a represented employee is inconsistent with the principles of working with the employee-complainant to ensure his or her protection from harassment and retaliation.

For all of these reasons, it is best to evaluate the best methods for soliciting and handling harassment complaints when your organization has a formal grievance process in place. Consult legal counsel regarding the appropriate use of grievance provisions for harassment complaints.

Co-workers may shun complainants or respondents during an investigation, especially when one of the parties in the complaint is well liked.

To protect employees from retaliation, be conscientious about establishing and following a complaint procedure for possible retaliation. To cover situations when unit supervisors or managers are alleged to have been involved in the harassment, you may need to establish a special complaint procedure that bypasses the normal reporting channels. For example, during an investigation of complaints about a workgroup that has been accused of fostering a hostile environment, a complaint procedure could be established that does not involve any of the unit managers.

At the outset of any investigation, HR also should remind supervisors to assign work fairly and carefully to ensure that no differences arise after a complaint is filed or a witness participates in an investigation interview. Even when retaliation is not a factor, the employees involved in a harassment investigation generally find the process personally stressful. They may seek specific reassurances from you about the outcome of the investigation. Your natural response to a highly emotional employee may be to give reassurance that everything will be all right, but you will not be able to give such assurances when you are investigating a harassment complaint. Because you represent the organization and are not an advocate for any party to the complaint, you must preserve the objectivity of the investigation at all times. Avoid conferring approval to a respondent by reassuring him or her that everything will be all right in the end. Similarly, while you want to document the complaint (see Chapter 6), it is not a good idea to write a file note every time a complainant approaches you with a noncomplaint inquiry. The complainant could experience this as retaliatory and indeed, it might be.

Challenges for the Investigator

You may find that being in the role of the investigator often is a thankless task. The work is hard but unappreciated. Some HR work gives you the opportunity to achieve "win-win" outcomes. Rarely will you completely satisfy even one of the parties in a harassment complaint, much less both.

Relationships with Colleagues

Concerns about confidentiality usually prevent employees from being told all the relevant information. As a result, employees tend to form factions. You may even become a scapegoat for employees who—not knowing the whole story—are unhappy with the outcome of the investigation. An investigator must therefore develop a thick skin and be unconcerned about being well liked and popular. In extreme situations, companies may find it prudent to use external investigators to avoid polarizing the relationship between HR and various employee factions. Other reasons to use an external investigator are discussed in Chapter 4.

As an investigator, you may find yourself in the awkward position of having to be the spokesperson for work rules that some employees find rigid or invasive. Most HR professionals don't enjoy getting in the way of employees' collegiality—of their having legitimate fun. Unfortunately, popular television situation comedies often depict the workplace as one big party. The growing trend toward increasing informality in today's workplaces helps foster the illusion that "anything goes." Joking around about potentially offensive subjects or taunting co-workers with innuendo pose unacceptable risks of liability to the organization under laws that protect employees from harassment. Also, these jokes rarely are humorous to many, if not most, employees. HR is charged with overseeing compliance with the law. Thus, your duty requires you to conduct a thorough and appropriate investigation while attempting to preserve positive working relationships and avoid sending the message that employees cannot enjoy themselves at work.

The Investigator's Mindset

Witnesses frequently "line up" to support one or the other side in conflicts involving their co-workers. You must be able to listen and question without taking sides or trying to fix the situation. Therapists are trained in how to listen to this sort of information without becoming personally involved or overwhelmed. Investigators rarely have this training and must develop their own methods for coping with the feelings that arise from listening to intense emotions. This is another reason to use outside "professional investigators" when the situation is particularly intense.

When you take on the role of investigator, you temporarily leave behind many of the methods of achieving cooperation and preserving good relationships that are HR's stock in trade. You will have to adopt a style that probes what people say with the critical perspective necessary to uncover an accurate version of events. In another context, you might encourage an employee to overlook his or her negative reaction to a co-worker in the interest of a harmonious work unit. In the context of an investigation, you will actively solicit all the reasons that led an employee to conclude that he or she is being harassed. If you are a relatively inexperienced investigator, you may find it helpful to consult the sample interviews that are in the appendices and focus on the specific advice for interviewing that is presented in Chapter 7.

Employees may notice a difference from your usual demeanor when you are working on an investigation. Because you are focused wholly on the investigation and must maintain impartiality, you may bypass opportunities you otherwise would take to coach a manager or supervisor regarding an employee problem.

Be prepared for questions to arise when employees notice your behavior has changed. It is likely that your future dealings with employees you encounter in the investigation will not immediately return to what they were before you investigated the complaint. You may be able to ease this transition somewhat by explaining to the employees how your role differs in these circumstances.

Figure 4 presents a list of typical challenges faced by investigators.

Figure 4. Typical Challenges for the Investigator

Before you begin an investigation, assess your available time and energy for some difficult, embarrassing, and awkward communication. You will be talking about intimate matters with employees whom you may have known only superficially. Your role as the investigator will require you to

- learn about the normal interactions and jargon among workers in the workgroup;
- listen with sensitivity to the way others perceive interpersonal exchanges;
- think objectively about how a person can be offended by conduct that you may see as innocent and harmless;
- carefully observe body language and other cues that may communicate important messages;
- listen to and repeat profane, disparaging or sexually explicit language;
- take in stride challenges to your competency and implied criticism of your ability to be neutral and objective;
- manage interviews with employees at varying levels in the organization's hierarchy, perhaps including people who outrank you;
- understand why a complainant or witness would not tell someone about things that happened;
- listen patiently while a complainant or witness unburdens him or herself of months or even years of accumulated hurtful memories;
- obtain answers to important questions from witnesses who may be determined to obfuscate their role in a situation;
- be assertive in discussions, repeating an important question as many times as it takes to get a straightforward, understandable answer;
- follow through consistently and practice exemplary organization in keeping track of notes and documents and in fulfilling commitments to important deadlines; and
- perfect your analytical thinking and critical reasoning to evaluate conflicting and often ambiguous witness accounts of incidents.

Emotional Intelligence

Researchers have identified differences among people in their capacity to recognize and respond to emotional stimuli within themselves and from other people. Psychologist Daniel Goleman's books about "emotional intelligence" have introduced this concept to the public.[1] Goleman and other writers have challenged the idea that mental capacity is limited to the kind of intelligence that is measured by an IQ test. Proponents of the concept of emotional intelligence assert that without attending to cues and feelings from sources other than our intellect, we are unable to adequately size up situations among people.

Your effectiveness as an investigator depends on preparing yourself to recognize and follow up on data about the emotional content of a given situation or incident. Your own emotional intelligence will come into play in two ways. You will need to cultivate a heightened awareness of your own emotional responses to what you see and hear, and you will need to observe the people you interview with sensitivity.

It helps to understand the importance of emotional data and the contrast between these "subjective impressions" and what many people think of as the purely rational data processed by the intellect. Investigators may be fearful of weighing witness' emotional reactions when, it seems, the easier way would be to reach a logical conclusion derived from a rational process that does not depend on understanding a person's emotional state. In harassment situations, however—as in other parts of our lives—emotions form an important component of experience. Thus, the emotional aspects of a harassment complaint cannot be ignored. Rather, they should be another arena for gathering and understanding information.

In your investigation, you are likely to find that complainants, respondents, and witnesses have a hard time articulating how their own emotional intelligence influenced the way they experienced an incident or colored the way they related to another person. Likewise, your own emotional intelligence will give you important cues about the parties to the complaint that you must try to understand and put into words.

It may be helpful to think about peoples' behavior on first meeting as an analogy for what you will often encounter when you investigate harassment complaints. Consider the signals that often accompany exchanges between two people who are meeting and talking for the first time. The way the parties position their bodies—how closely they stand or sit, whether one or both parties leans toward or touches the other person, how steadily they maintain eye contact—these and other signals all carry clues about each party's comfort level, degree of interest in the other person, and involvement in the discussion or interaction.

In such a situation, the parties use their emotional intelligence to gather clues about each other. How comfortable does the other person seem? Is he or she under stress or calm, composed or distracted, approachable or distant? Each party's instincts in this regard will often—though not always—be accurate. Nonetheless, it may be difficult for either person to put into words the reasons for his or her assessment of the other person or their interaction.

Example #1

Annabella and Phillip

Annabella, a smoker, has joined the HR group as a receptionist. Phillip, the office network administrator, frequently joins Annabella during her smoking breaks. Annabella notices that Phillip stands closer to her than he does to the other employees who are smoking on the patio. Annabella feels uncomfortable; is Phillip's attention a clue that something else is going on? Annabella tells herself not to be concerned because Phillip probably is just being nice to a new employee. A few times, Annabella feels that Phillip asks her questions that are too personal. But she discounts her concerns because she knows that Phillip is married.

One day when Phillip is out on sick leave, a female co-worker, also a fellow smoker, asks Annabella if she is "getting tired of Phillip hitting on you yet?" The co-worker explains that Phillip "has a thing" for younger, single women employees. The co-worker says, "Phillip has worked here for nine years but he never smoked before you started coming out here on breaks."

Annabella immediately goes back to the department and speaks to her supervisor, the HR manager, about Phillip and what she has learned from the co-worker.

The HR manager isn't sure that an investigation is necessary because the only fact Annabella can articulate that suggests harassment is that Phillip has stood close to her on the patio. The HR manager's quick dismissal of Annabella's concerns ignores what Annabella has learned by employing her emotional intelligence. The HR manager has no comparable emotional information because he has never seen anything unusual in Phillip's behavior.

The HR manager's decision to discount Annabella's complaint denies the organization the opportunity to learn important information. By making a decision based only on his own experience, the HR manager may miss something important. Instead, he should explore Annabella's response so that he can understand Phillip's conduct from her perspective. To do this, the HR manager might ask, "What did you feel was happening between you and Phillip?" or "What was different about Phillip's attention than other co-worker's attention which led you to complain?"

Without investigating Annabella's complaint, the organization won't gain the information it needs to fairly evaluate the complaint's validity. Such an investigation might reveal that other women have been victims of Phillip's improper advances. Alternatively, a thorough investigation might reveal no prior incidents and that Phillip—though perhaps clumsy or even inappropriate in his attempts to befriend Annabella—actually has no predatory motive. At the very least, an investigation here should reveal that Phillip has been standing closer to Annabella than he does to other employees and that he has changed his behavior (became a smoker), perhaps to give him an opportunity to be closer to her. This behavior may not violate any employer rules, but it clearly (and legitimately) has made Annabella uncomfortable—so it needs to be addressed.

As an investigator, you will use your emotional intelligence to notice and probe deeper when a party expresses a higher or lower level of distress than a situation, on its face, seems to warrant. Your emotional intelligence will assist you in investigating each matter appropriately and help prevent you from missing things that lie beneath the surface. Remember that without a fair and thorough investigation, the organization will not have sufficient information to draw an accurate conclusion or take appropriate remedial actions.

Benefits of Conducting Investigations

A well-planned and carefully conducted investigation will produce information that can completely "clear the air" regarding potential or actual problems of harassment. The investigation will benefit the complainant because—perhaps for the first time—he or she will have the opportunity to fully state his or her complaints and the basis for each. Respondents who believe they have been unjustly accused also will benefit because the investigation will establish what problems did or didn't exist and the connection, if any, to organizational harassment policies. Co-workers who have observed a troubled work relationship learn that the organization takes such problems seriously and acts on them appropriately. From the organization's point of view, the investigation will conclusively establish the nature and extent of any problems raised by the complainant. An investigation also can reveal the extent of employee understanding of the organization's policies.

Chapter 1 Self-Check

This chapter has given you an overview of the issue of workplace harassment and challenges that may arise as you prepare for the investigation. To further your knowledge, consider the following questions. Where applicable, answers to self-check questions have been provided in Appendix A.

1. What are the factors in your employer's workforce that would make the reporting of prohibited harassment more or less likely?
2. What level of backing can you expect from your organization's operating units (for example, departments) in relation to providing the resources and leadership support that you will need to conduct an investigation? What can you do to increase the chances that operating units will back you?
3. What are the barriers in your organization to using emotional intelligence data to evaluate employee conflict? How can you overcome them?

Harassment and the Law

Before you embark on an investigation of workplace harassment you should understand the law prohibiting harassment and the relationship between an employer's policies and the law. Employers have obligations under various laws, contracts (such as union contracts), and their own policies to protect employees from harassment. Familiarity with the contents of published court decisions will give you ideas about what to look for during the investigation. Figure 5 shows the variety of different laws and contractual obligations, or "compliance influences," that may apply to a given employer.

Laws Prohibiting Workplace Harassment

State and federal laws prohibit discrimination in the workplace. Some municipalities also have passed laws that expand the categories of people protected from discrimination at work. Harassment is considered one form of discrimination. Therefore, discriminatory harassment violates these laws. Most state laws resemble the federal law and a state statute must provide at least as much protection against discrimination as the federal statute.

Some state anti-discrimination laws are even broader than the federal law. The differences between state and federal laws usually are unimportant when it comes to preventing and responding to harassment, but may affect when an employer may be held liable for harassment. For example, some states and municipalities have laws protecting employees from harassment based on sexual orientation whereas the federal law does not include sexual orientation among the protected categories.

Most employer policies afford broad protection under their nonharassment provisions. Whether the harassment relates to a protected category (such as race) or an unprotected category (such as wearing striped clothing),

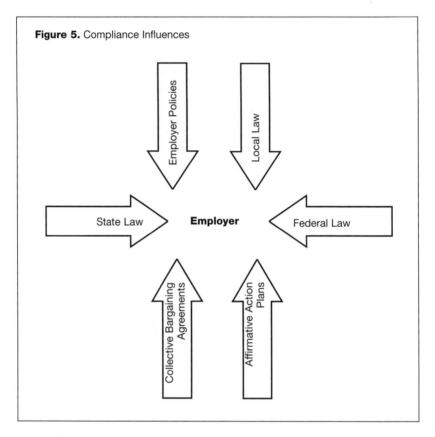

Figure 5. Compliance Influences

it's good HR practice to respond appropriately to all complaints of harassment.

To violate the law, harassment must

1. be based on a status protected by law, such as sex, race, religion, disability, sexual orientation (in some jurisdictions); and

2. be either *quid pro quo* sexual harassment or be severe or pervasive enough to alter the conditions of employment.

"*Quid pro quo*" is a Latin term that means "this for that." It refers to the type of sexual harassment that involves threatening to exchange or exchanging a tangible work benefit, such as a raise in pay or the chance to be promoted, for sexual favors or some other action.

The "severe or pervasive" standard, which applies to hostile work environment situations involving sexual harassment and all other forms of harassment, looks to the seriousness of the conduct. Only harassment that is determined to be severe or pervasive violates the law. Because of this standard, most isolated incidents—unless the incident is very severe—will not violate the law.

Under federal law a variety of laws protect employees from discrimination (including retaliation). These laws include Title VII of the Civil Rights Act of 1964, the Americans with Disabilities Act of 1990, the Age Discrimination in Employment Act of 1967, and the Family and Medical Leave Act. The categories that are protected under federal law include

- Race
- Sex (including pregnancy)
- Religion
- Color
- Age
- National origin
- Disability

In some states, counties, or cities, protections also extend to

- Marital status
- Sexual orientation
- Medical condition
- Physical appearance

Workplace rules that prohibit harassment—including sexual harassment—usually are broader than the law. Again, to violate the law, the conduct must be severe or pervasive. To violate internal workplace rules against harassment found in many organizational policy documents, the conduct need only be unwanted. For example, Paula Jones claimed that Bill Clinton, then governor of Arkansas (akin to being the state's CEO) invited her to his hotel room, exposed himself to her, and asked for sexual favors. Was this sexual harassment under the law? Not according to one federal court. Would such conduct have been a violation of most employers' rules prohibiting harassment? Almost certainly.

The Paula Jones case is an extreme example. To violate the law, the conduct must involve some tangible job benefit or else be ongoing or extreme. In other cases, courts have found that occasional references to race, even if they are derogatory, are not enough to violate the law. A California court found that calling an employee "Buckwheat" on one or two occasions and sporadic other remarks that the plaintiff found racially offensive were insufficient for a finding of racial harassment. (See *Etter -v- Veriflo Corp.*[2]) The court in the Etter case stated that to be actionable, racial harassment must be more than "occasional, isolated, sporadic, or trivial acts." Despite this ruling and other decisions in similar cases, we hope that most employers agree that the type of conduct that was alleged in the *Etter* case would violate workplace rules.

Predicting what behavior a judge or jury will determine to be sufficiently severe or pervasive to violate the law is very difficult. Furthermore, if left unchecked, harassment that begins innocuously can become pervasive or severe. These are some of many reasons that employers should respond to all harassment—even harassment that appears to be isolated or trivial.

In 1999 the Equal Employment Opportunity Commission (EEOC) promulgated regulations that provide guidance on when an employer is liable for unlawful harassment by supervisors. Based in part on two United States Supreme Court decisions in sexual harassment cases (*Burlington Industries -v- Ellerth* and *Faragher -v- City of Boca Raton*[3]), the regulations make it clear that the guidelines apply to all forms of workplace harassment that violate Title VII. The guidelines also provide extensive information on what is expected from employers in regard to the prevention of and response to harassment.

Unionized work settings may prohibit harassment in collective bargaining agreements (CBAs) or memoranda of understanding (MOUs) between the employer and the union. These documents form contractual obligations to treat harassment in certain ways. Affirmative Action plans also may include sections on harassment and how complaints must be handled. Employers should be aware of which laws and contractual obligations apply to them.

Definitions and Examples

As an investigator and an HR employee who must counsel other employees about your organization's policies, you need to have a clear understanding of the meanings of specific terms. What is harassment? What is discrimination? What is sexual harassment? Many of the terms you will encounter and use in an investigation have specific meanings as defined by law or by court interpretations.

Discrimination

Discrimination is treating people differently because they are members of a certain group. Discrimination is an action, not just an attitude. Having a prejudiced idea is not an action. A person can have a prejudice without engaging in actions that discriminate on the basis of that image or prejudice. For example, someone might have a mental image of doctors as being male (a sexist attitude—none of us is free from some of these ideas!) but still go to female doctors.

Attitudes are not always acted on and so do not necessarily result in discrimination. When a person in a position of authority makes a decision about some aspect of another person's employment because of a stereotype, however, prejudice moves from the realm of ideas and feelings into the realm of actions—and thus, potentially, discrimination. For example, a manager might believe that "older workers are less flexible—so they should be laid off first when our company experiences an economic downturn." If the manager decides to lay off older workers on the basis of this belief, the manager has discriminated against the older workers.

Unlawful Discrimination

Discrimination becomes unlawful if, in an employment setting, an individual is treated differently because he or she is a member of a protected category. The manager noted above has discriminated unlawfully against the older workers because the basis of his decision in the layoff is age, which is a protected category under federal law.

By contrast, consider a supervisor who dislikes people who wear stripes. The stripes look silly to this supervisor and she assumes that people who wear them are silly. She therefore does not assign important tasks to people who wear stripes.

This supervisor is discriminating. But wearing stripes is not indicative of being a member of a protected group. The discrimination, though unfair, is not illegal. Of course, this does not mean such discrimination is okay. At the very least, it constitutes poor supervision!

Harassment

Harassment occurs when the discriminatory behavior is the manner in which an employee is treated or spoken to, rather than the terms and conditions of employment. As defined above, to be unlawful, harassment must be severe or pervasive. Unlawful harassment based on race often occurs in the form of racial epithets and the telling of jokes that are disrespectful to a racial or ethnic group. As explained above, unless it is severe, a single instance of joke-telling or a single use of an epithet probably is insufficient to make the harassment meet the criteria for being unlawful. There must be a pattern, persistence, or severity to make the harassing behavior unlawful, but harassment need not rise to a standard of unlawfulness to be unacceptable in the workplace.

Sexual Harassment

Simply defined, sexual harassment is when the harassment is sexual, such as sexual jokes, innuendos, requests for dates, and so forth. The harassment can be verbal, physical, or even visual.

Some examples of sexual harassment include

- pressure for sexual favors,
- touching,
- cornering,
- suggestive letters or calls,
- pressure for dates,
- suggestive looks,
- sexual teasing, jokes, remarks, and
- gestures.

The two elements that must be present for behavior to constitute sexual harassment are

1. the behavior must be unwelcome, and
2. the behavior must be of a sexual nature.

The law defines sexual harassment in very specific terms. As stated above, legal liability for sexual harassment is limited to specific situations; however, an employer must necessarily use a broader definition in policies and procedures in order to prevent offensive behavior.

Legal Definition of Sexual Harassment

In the 1980s the EEOC issued guidelines defining sexual harassment. The guidelines are found at 29 Code of Federal Regulations Section 1604.11. In 1986 the United States Supreme Court approved this definition in *Meritor Savings Bank -v- Vinson*.[4] Since then, this definition has been quoted frequently as the legal definition of sexual harassment. It appears in countless court decisions and often is quoted in employer policies. The definition is "unwelcome sexual advances, requests for sexual favors, and other verbal or physical conduct of a sexual nature constitute sexual harassment when

1. submission to such conduct is made either explicitly or implicitly a term or condition of an individual's employment,
2. submission to or rejection of such conduct by an individual is used as the basis for employment decisions affecting such individual, or
3. such conduct has the purpose or effect of unreasonably interfering with an individual's work performance or creating an intimidating, hostile, or offensive work environment."

The first two prongs of this three-pronged definition refer to *quid pro quo* harassment. The third prong refers to the "hostile work environment" type of harassment. Of course, some claims of sexual harassment will include allegations of both *quid pro quo* harassment and hostile work environment harassment.

Again, workplace rules that prohibit harassment—including sexual harassment—usually are broader than the law. In order to violate internal workplace rules against harassment, such conduct need only be unwanted.

Gender-Based Harassment

Gender-based harassment (also called "sex-based harassment") is due to the employee's gender but is not overtly sexual. Examples may include behavior like excluding women from meetings, making statements that demean women, teasing women about not being as strong as men, or putting frogs in a woman's locker. This sort of harassment often happens when people of one gender work in an environment predominately composed of people of the other gender—such as a woman working on a construction crew or a male nurse.

Example #2

Lucy and the Construction Crew

Lucy is the only female employee on a construction crew. During her lunch breaks no one will sit with her. Instead, the male workers walk by her, making comments about women staying at home. **The foreman assigns Lucy the most difficult tasks and will not team her up with anyone, as he does for the male workers. When Lucy complains, her co-workers say they are teasing and she is overly sensitive. The foreman says he has just been testing her mettle, as he does to all new employees.**

Here Lucy has been subjected to harassment. If indeed all new employees are treated this way, the harassment may not be gender-based. It will certainly seem that way to Lucy, however, and the statements about women staying at home are direct evidence of gender bias.

Same-Sex Sexual Harassment

Harassment is conduct; the gender of the parties involved is irrelevant. Most workplace harassment is male to female. According to EEOC statistics, in 1992, males filed 9.1% of the sexual harassment charges that were filed with the EEOC and state and local Fair Employment Practices agencies around the country. This figure has increased slightly every year. In 2001 the percentage of charges filed by men was 13.7%. The percentage reflects both societal norms (men usually are expected to be the aggressor in intimate relations) and workplace norms (men usually have more organizational power than women). As these norms change, the way sexual harassment is played out at work probably will also change.

Harassment also occurs from females to males, males to males, and females to females. All these forms of harassment are prohibited and the same standards should be applied to allegations of same-sex sexual harassment as to harassment between a male and a female. Same-sex harassment does not depend on the sexual orientation of any party. For example, a heterosexual male could be harassed by another heterosexual male and it could still constitute sexual harassment.

In *Oncale -v- Sundowner Offshore Servs., Inc.*, the Supreme Court determined that same-sex sexual harassment violates antidiscrimination laws when it is motivated by the individual's gender.[5] It is difficult to predict when same-sex sexual harassment will be considered based on gender as opposed to some other reason. Therefore, the investigator should not be concerned with what a court of law will do but rather should focus on whether the behavior violates work rules prohibiting harassment. Also, remember that while most sexual harassment is male to female, a female can harass a male.

Impact versus Intent

In harassment situations the harassment is evaluated based on the recipient's response rather than the perpetrator's intentions. If a reasonable person would find the conduct offensive, the fact that the perpetrator would not does not absolve that individual of responsibility. An employer can be held liable for harassment (and actions can violate an employer's rules) even if the person engaging in the behavior meant no harm. This is why some experts in the field say the issue is the impact rather than the intent. Of course, not all actions that are considered harassment are equally serious. A boorish individual who is trying to amuse but instead offends generally will not be disciplined as severely as someone who intentionally tries to hurt someone. Intent is a relevant factor that the investigator will want to understand, to the extent possible, so that the actions can be placed in the proper context. But the absence of any bad intent does not absolve employees of responsibility for violating employer rules against harassment. This concept clearly applies in third-party harassment situations, which are discussed next.

Third-Party Harassment

Third-party harassment occurs when two individuals engage in consensual talk or conduct that affects a third party who does not welcome the behavior. This kind of harassment generally comes up in the context of sexual harassment when two or more co-workers enjoy engaging in sexual joking or conversation and do so with others present. While this sort of behavior seldom is severe and may not involve a specific target for the harassment, it can contribute to an environment of harassment at work because one or more of the noninvolved co-workers may become offended. Also, the conduct clearly is unprofessional. Even though the conduct is welcome between the participants, it should be stopped.

Retaliation

When a person reports or participates in someone else's report of harassment, he or she is protected from any form of retaliation. In order to violate the law, the retaliation must meet a certain legal threshold. But it is difficult to predict what a court will do. It is good HR practice to make sure all employees know retaliation is prohibited and to promptly respond to any complaint of retaliation. Many sexual harassment lawsuits come about because of the complainant's perception that the employer retaliated against him or her after he or she brought forward the complaint. The retaliation may take the form of being mistreated (such as shunned by co-workers) or it may be a demotion or termination. Remember, there need not be a determination that unlawful harassment has occurred for the anti-retaliation provisions to apply.

Example #3

Franklin's Termination

Franklin makes a complaint of racial harassment based on a joke told during his employer's training class. After making his complaint, Franklin is not promoted because he is thought to be a troublemaker. Shortly thereafter, he is fired. An outside investigator is asked to investigate Franklin's complaint. The investigator determines that the behavior Franklin had complained about was isolated and therefore a minor violation of the employer's harassment-free workplace policy, warranting counseling for the person responsible. But the investigator also finds that the failure to promote Franklin and his termination of employment occurred in retaliation for his complaining, which warrants serious disciplinary action against the supervisor responsible for the termination.

Franklin's situation illustrates that a retaliation charge does not depend on the underlying harassment charge. Even if the investigator determines that Franklin misinterpreted the joke and there was no violation of the employer's policy, failing to promote and later terminating Franklin because of his complaint clearly was improper. The independence of retaliation-related charges also holds true when employees complain about practices that do not involve harassment but that they believe violate the law, such as discriminatory work assignments.

When the Complainant and Respondent Have Dated

The fact that a complainant and respondent once dated should not deter you from investigating. Many legitimate sexual harassment complaints arise from situations where the parties once dated but one party has ended the relationship. What happens outside of work is generally none of the employer's business. But when such a situation negatively affects relationships at work, the employer must become involved.

Employer Policies and Compliance with the Law

The necessity for clearly written policies prohibiting workplace harassment has long been recognized. For many years, good human resource practice has included the regular distribution and explanation of such policies—and their consistent enforcement. The *Faragher* and *Ellerth* cases further established the importance of such policies. In these cases, the Supreme Court held that employers will not be held liable for harassment by supervisors that does not involve the loss of a tangible job benefit if

- the employer has adequate policies and procedures to prevent harassment, and
- the victim of the harassment unreasonably failed to use these procedures.

In applying these cases, lower courts have found that the mere existence of an employer policy prohibiting harassment is not enough to shield the employer from liability. To work as a shield, the policy must be adequate and it must be distributed to employees.

Employer policies should protect employees from harassment by employees *and* nonemployees—including, for example, vendors and customers. Legal precedent and good HR practice dictate that the employer is responsible for protecting employees from harassment regardless of the source.

As stated above, employer policies usually prohibit a broader range of behavior than does the law. If an employer waits until conduct violates the law before taking disciplinary action, harassment would be tolerated—which undermines the law. The point of employer policies and actions regarding harassment is to stop the harassment before it becomes sufficiently severe and pervasive to violate the law.

Effective policies include not only written policies, but also explanations of those policies to all employees and training for supervisors and managers on how to recognize harassment and respond to complaints of harassment. They also include effective prevention plans that prevent harassment from occurring and provide training in how to respond to harassment that does occur before it gets serious. Implementing an effective policy protects the employer and its employees from being found liable for harassment. It also is the right thing to do!

A written policy should be given to all employees. The policy should be thorough and easy to understand. HR should periodically republish the policy and include it in all new-employee orientations. When employees are hired or promoted to supervisory positions, HR should hold a training meeting with them to review their new responsibilities under the employer's harassment-free workplace policy.

Under some state laws an anti-harassment policy must include certain information. Additionally, all employers who are subject to Title VII of the Civil Rights Act of 1964 and many other employers (depending on the state where their facilities are located) must post notices regarding harassment. You will find a sample of a state model policy in Appendix B. A listing of fair employment agencies by state is at the web site www.hrdocument.com/investigations/feplisting.html.

The EEOC Guidance on Vicarious Employer Liability for Unlawful Harassment by Supervisors, promulgated in 1999, sets forth the minimum elements for an anti-harassment policy and complaint procedure. These guidelines state that a policy should contain

■ a clear explanation of prohibited conduct;
■ assurance that employees who make complaints of harassment or provide information related to such complaints will be protected against retaliation;
■ a clearly described complaint process that provides accessible avenues of complaint;
■ assurance that the employer will protect the confidentiality of harassment complaints to the extent possible;
■ a complaint process that provides a prompt, thorough, and impartial investigation; and
■ assurance that the employer will take immediate and appropriate corrective action when it determines that harassment has occurred.

Most effective employer policies also will include

■ the legal definition of sexual harassment (usually the definition set forth above);
■ descriptions of sexual harassment, gender-based harassment, and other types of workplace harassment, with examples;
■ the name and telephone number of the employee to whom complaints can be made, including an 800 number if the contact person is out of state; and
■ if required by state law, the legal remedies and complaint process available through the EEOC and state fair employment agencies, along with information on how to contact these agencies.

Some, but not all, states require the policy to include information about the legal remedies and the complaint process available through the EEOC or state agency. Many employers will not include this information if it is not required in the states where they do business. It is done with more frequency, however, and it is beginning to be considered good practice even where it is not required. When feasible, it also is a good idea to provide both male and female contacts to accept harassment complaints.

Most employers do not have a mechanism in place for ensuring that all complaints are truly confidential. If confidentiality is desired one way an organization can encourage confidential reporting is by using an ombudsperson reporting system (Figure 6).

Some lawsuits have resulted in courts ordering employers to enact policies and procedures specific to sexual harassment. In *Robinson -v- Jack-*

Figure 6. When Can a Complaint of Harassment Be Kept Confidential? Using an Ombudsperson for Investigating Complaints

Employers generally agree that they must act on complaints of harassment, whether they are formally filed complaints, rumor, or anonymous sources. For one thing, an employer is liable for harassment if the employer knew or should have known about the harassment but failed to act.

Unfortunately, the employer's mandate to act effectively blocks the complainant from anonymity. Some employers believe that if complaints cannot be kept confidential, some complaints will never surface—and hence will never be attended to. Using an ombudsperson for intake of harassment complaints and for informal resolution of such complaints provides one method for shielding harassment complaints with a veil of confidentiality.

An ombudsperson can be a resource for receiving and informally resolving complaints. An ombudsperson functions outside the typical chains of command within the organization—at least with respect to these particular duties. Policies clearly set out that complaints can be made to the ombudsperson and will remain confidential unless the employee agrees otherwise. The ombudsperson is usually highly trained and is empowered to work with the employee and try to help him or her resolve the concerns raised by the complaint. Doing this often leads to getting agreement to reveal the complaint. However, if the employee insists it remain confidential, this position is honored and the organization receives no notice of the complaint. Employers who provide an ombudsman system almost always have a parallel track for employees who do want to file formal complaints.

sonville Shipyards, Inc., a Florida court specifically approved of a detailed written policy (as well as ordering training and investigations of complaints).[6] The policies and parameters of the training are set forth in an appendix to the court's decision and are instructive.

How Employer Policies Affect Legal Liability

Many courts throughout the country have found that an employer's effective policy prohibiting harassment can have an impact on liability. Most of these cases involve claims of sexual harassment, but in some cases courts have applied this to other forms of harassment and discrimination. The existence and utilization of policies can lead to an employer avoiding any liability for workplace harassment, as described in the *Faragher* and *Ellerth* cases. Good policies can also help employers avoid exposure to punitive damages.

Just as good policies can prevent liability, bad policies can increase it. The case of *Weeks -v- Baker & MacKenzie* received nationwide attention because it involved a legal secretary suing the largest law firm in the United States.[7] As sexual harassment cases go, the facts were not very egregious. But the plaintiff showed that the law firm knew about the harassment and failed to act. This resulted in a relatively small jury verdict for the plaintiff's emotional distress ($150,000) but a huge verdict of punitive damages against the law firm ($6.9 million). The punitive damages against the law firm later were cut by the court to $3.5 million.

Responding to Harassment

The critical importance of an immediate response to all incidents of workplace harassment cannot be overstated. Responding immediately and clearly benefits everyone at work. The victim benefits because the conduct is not allowed to continue and he or she is taken seriously. The workgroup benefits because employees see a clear and consistent message that harassment is inappropriate. Perpetrators also benefit because they learn immediately what conduct is inappropriate and why. Perpetrators then have an opportunity to correct their behavior and not repeat the harassment.

The Cost of Not Responding

Harassment that is not addressed often is repeated—and usually worsens. As harassment grows worse, the damage to the victim also grows. If the behavior becomes sufficiently severe, the perpetrator loses his or her job. Moreover, the longer harassment is not addressed, the greater the risk that the organization will be perceived to have tolerated the behavior. This perception puts the organization at risk.

Statistics show that most victims don't complain about harassment. Supervisors should receive training about their responsibility to prevent, recognize, and respond to harassment regardless of whether it is reported.

Supervisor's Responsibilities

Supervisors and managers have a high level of responsibility in promoting and enforcing anti-harassment policies. They must act as role models and not engage in harassment. They also must be able to recognize harassment and respond appropriately. While employees can be apprised of policies against harassment, supervisors and managers will need lengthier training to ensure that policies are properly enforced. Such training should cover the supervisor's duties to

- monitor the work environment;
- know and explain the organization's harassment-free workplace policy;
- respond to known harassment; and
- appropriately accept complaints.

Supervisors need to be clear about the organization's commitment to a harassment-free workplace and their role in carrying out that commitment. For example, supervisors who observe behavior that could be problematic must know that they should not wait for someone involved to complain.

Most employers don't want supervisors conducting investigations of workplace harassment. Rarely do supervisors have adequate training and experience, nor can they spare the time from their regular duties. Employers want supervisors to be available if an employee comes to them with a complaint and to know enough about the policies and procedures to pass the complaint on to the right person on a timely basis. Many lawsuits have come about because an untrained supervisor took things into his or her own hands.

Supervisors sometimes try to limit the amount of information that their subordinates report to HR or other higher level managers. Supervisors who instruct their employees not to share information about complaints of harassment can create significant liability for the employer when the unreported problems eventually come to light in litigation. Once a supervisor has informed HR about a potential problem, he or she should not take any more action without advice from HR.

Anti-harassment Training

Employees can be apprised of policies against harassment at orientations and other meetings. Supervisors and managers need lengthier training to ensure that policies are properly enforced. Such training should cover the supervisor's duties to: monitor the work environment; know and explain the harassment policy; respond to known harassment; and appropriately accept complaints.

A new legal trend is to mandate that employers provide such training. Maine requires sexual harassment training for new employees and for supervisors at workplaces with more than 15 employees. (*See* Me. Rev. Stat. Sec. 807(3).) Connecticut mandates effective and interactive training for supervisors who work for employers with more than 50 employees (*See* Conn. Gen Stat. Sec 46a-54(15)(B); Conn. Agencies Regs. Sec. 46a-54-204.) California mandates a minimum of two hours of interactive sexual harassment training for supervisors/managers at workplaces with more than 50 employees (*See* Calif. Gov't Code Sec. 12950.1)

Chapter 2 Self-Check

This chapter has presented information about major legal concepts and precedents related to workplace harassment. To further your knowledge, consider the following questions. Where applicable, answers have been provided in Appendix A. Other answers will depend on details particular to your organization.

1. Is harassment always unlawful? If not, what is the difference between harassment that does and does not violate the law?
2. How can employers protect themselves from legal liability for harassment? (Take a look at your own organization. Are your policies current and are employees aware of them? Are there steps you could take to improve your organization's prevention plan?)

CHAPTER 3

Investigations and the Law

Some lawsuits center on the employer's response to a complaint of discriminatory harassment. In these situations, the employer's entire investigation is put under scrutiny. An employee may claim that he or she was harassed and the employer took inadequate action. Alternatively, an employee who has been disciplined for harassment may claim that the investigation of the complaint was unfair or inadequate.

In the first instance, the complainant could file a lawsuit asserting that the investigation of his or her harassment claim was insufficient or unfair—and thus that the actions the employer took as a result of the investigation also were insufficient or unfair. In the second instance, the employee against whom the complaint was filed could file a lawsuit claiming libel or, if he or she was fired as the result of the investigation, wrongful termination. Note that no separate legal claim exists for an inadequate investigation. Rather, the issue comes up within a broader claim of unlawful harassment, libel, or wrongful termination.

These concepts also may arise in other types of legal or quasi-legal proceedings. For example, an employee terminated for harassment may apply for unemployment benefits and the employer may want to respond without forcing witnesses to testify. Using statements from an investigation or the investigator's testimony may be sufficient evidence for a finding that the employee was discharged for misconduct and hence the employer not responsible for his or her unemployment benefits. If an employee has the right to a hearing for disciplinary action (this usually applies to public employees and unionized employees but also could apply to private employers with grievance policies or arbitration clauses) issues concerning the investigation will no doubt arise.

Lawsuits by Complainants

Some lawsuits have determined liability and granted damages due to an employer's failure to adequately prevent or respond to harassment. In these cases the employee who brings the action must first prove that unlawful harassment took place. Once that is proven, the employer may find itself liable for the harassment, and damages may be significant if the complainant can show that the employer's response was inadequate. *Kimzey -v- Wal-Mart Stores, Inc.* resulted in a $50 million verdict against Wal-Mart (reduced to $350,000 on appeal).[8] In holding that punitive damages were warranted, the appellate court specifically noted the failure of management officials to investigate complaints of sexual harassment. In *Coates -v- Wal-Mart Stores, Inc.*, punitive damages of $1.75 million were upheld because of the employer's failure to adequately prevent and investigate harassment.[9]

In *Fuller -v- City of Oakland*, the court criticized the employer's investigation for failing to

- interview the accused promptly;
- corroborate the allegations (when it would have been easy to do so);
- interview an important witness for the complainant; and
- give sufficient weight to evidence in the complainant's favor.[10]

The inadequate investigation was the primary basis for the court's finding that the employer had failed to take appropriate remedial steps in response to a complaint of harassment.

Lawsuits by Respondents

Employers often believe that they are in a no-win situation when it comes to investigations of workplace harassment. If the employer doesn't find that the harassment took place—or if the employer takes too lenient an action against the alleged harasser—the complainant might sue the employer. But if the employer finds that the harassment occurred and terminates the respondent, the respondent might sue! Respondents have been known to bring charges against employers for

- defamation,
- violation of privacy rights, and
- wrongful termination.

Although unlikely, it also is possible that an employer whose investigation included heavy-handed tactics might even be charged with false imprisonment. Each of these charges has a specific basis in the law and each type of charge may be avoided or defeated if the investigation is pursued with care and diligence.

Defamation

Defamation consists of false statements that put an individual in a bad light. Generally, written statements of this sort are called "libel" and oral statements of this sort are called "slander." Repeating false statements (which could occur in the course of an investigation) can be considered defamation under certain circumstances. The possibility of a defamation complaint against your employer is one reason you must maintain confidentiality, limiting the exchange of information about your investigations to those individuals who need to know.

In most defamation lawsuits that arise out of an employer's investigation, there is a significant defense that will result in a finding of no liability for the employer. The law applies a concept called "qualified immunity" to good-faith investigations of workplace harassment. This means that an action for libel or slander will not succeed if the employer can show that the investigation was done reasonably and in good faith. As highlighted in *Ghebreselassie -v- Coleman Sec. Service*, this immunity applies to employers' investigations of personnel actions and employee conduct.[11] In *Cuenca -v- Safeway S.F. Employees Fed. Credit Union*, the plaintiff—who had been terminated based on allegations of potential criminal acts—could not proceed with a civil lawsuit for defamation because the court found that the employer had immunity based on there being no evidence that the employer had failed to act reasonably or had acted with malice.[12]

On the other hand, as shown by *Miller -v- City of West Columbia*, if the party bringing the lawsuit can show that the investigation was done in bad faith (or with what some courts call "malice"), the employer will have no such immunity.[13] In *Miller* the only evidence of sexual harassment was the complainant's statement, and she had failed a lie detector test. There was also evidence that the individual who decided to take action against the respondent had serious doubts as to the truthfulness of the allegations. When the respondent sued the employer, the court found that the employer had not acted reasonably and in good faith and was therefore not immune from the defamation charge.

Another important concept in defamation law is "self-publication"— a situation in which someone is forced to repeat defamatory statements about himself or herself. Self-publication could occur if someone is fired for harassment and then must tell prospective employers the reason he or she was separated from his or her last job. The employer faces tension between the desire to be clear about why an employee was terminated, and wanting to protect itself against a potential claim of defamation. This risk has led some employers to discharge employees for the less-specific reason of "violating work rules" rather than labeling it "harassment." At times, however, an employer will want to make a clear statement about why someone was disciplined. One reason to specify the reasons for discipline is the importance of accuracy. Should the employer have to deal with future legal actions, such as unemployment claims or lawsuits, this accuracy will be important. Accuracy also is important to be sure that the disciplined employee clearly understands why he or she has been disciplined and other employees know what actions will lead to discipline. It also may be important to the complainant that a determination that harassment occurred be communicated to the perpetrator. Employers should use the same care and discretion for disciplinary decisions regarding harassment as they do in other personnel matters.

Violation of Privacy Rights

An employee accused of harassment could file an action based on a violation of privacy rights if the accusations or findings have been communicated to others. Unlike defamation cases, in an action for violation of privacy rights the party bringing the action need not prove that the information communicated is false. As in defamation actions, however, the employer has a qualified immunity. In *Castleberry -v- Boeing Co.*, an employer that told more than 250 managers and supervisors the plaintiff was fired for sexual harassment was found not liable for violating the plaintiff's privacy rights because the employer had a legitimate interest in communicating the information to its workforce so that employees would be aware of the seriousness of the acts.[14] The communication was subject to a qualified immunity (also called a "privilege"), and the privilege was found not to have been abused.

Wrongful Termination

An employee discharged for harassment also may file a claim for wrongful termination. Some (but not all) states recognize this type of action. The viability of the claim also may depend on whether an employee is employed by a public employer, has a contract (through a union or other collective bargaining entity) and the employer's general course of conduct in administering discipline. But even when an employer is prohibited from discharging an employee without "good cause," an employer may discharge an employee for harassment based on a reasonable investigation conducted in good faith. Serious harassment almost always is considered good cause for a discharge.

A reasonable good-faith investigation protects the employer from liability for wrongful termination even if the investigator comes to the "wrong" conclusion. In *Cotran -v- Rollins Hudig Hall Intl, Inc.*, the employer fired an employee for sexual harassment.[15] The employee then sued the employer for wrongful termination, stating that he had not harassed the woman who had complained but in fact had ended an affair with her and she was a "spurned lover." Although he had the opportunity during the investigation, the employee had not told the employer this information. A jury found for the employee. The appellate court reversed the decision, however, finding that the employer's investigation had been conducted in good faith and had reasonably determined that the conduct occurred—and that, therefore, the employer could not be held liable for wrongful termination.

Another California case, *Silva -v- Lucky Stores, Inc.*, sets forth an example of what that court believed a reasonable investigation contains.[16] In *Silva* the court also found that an employee fired for sexual harassment could not succeed in a wrongful termination suit when there had been an appropriate investigation with a reasonable finding that the harassment had occurred. In making its determination, the court looked to various factors, including whether

- the investigator was neutral and had been trained;
- the investigator interviewed the alleged harasser and the victim and interviewed all pertinent witnesses;
- the investigator reviewed all relevant documents;
- the investigator documented the investigation and prepared a written report; and
- the investigator communicated the findings in a confidential manner to the interested parties.

The *Silva* decision included a statement to the effect that while the investigation was not perfect, it was appropriate given that it was conducted "under the exigencies of the workaday world and without benefit of the slow-moving machinery of a contested trial." The words of the court in the *Silva* case should provide a good deal of reassurance to investigators. Your investigation need not be perfect. No doubt, at times, you will fail to discover some facts. But if you are neutral, fair, and thorough, your investigation should be adequate.

False Imprisonment

Courts have reviewed workplace investigations from the perspective of the civil rights of the persons who are interviewed. Tactics of intimidation, such as restricting the ability of the interviewee to leave the interview room, have been the subject of criticism—and expensive damage awards—by judges and juries. The basis for these lawsuits is a tort called "false imprisonment." Most cases of false imprisonment in employment have involved the interrogation of employees accused of theft or fraud; however, it is possible that a heavy-handed investigation of a harassment complaint could lead to a charge of false imprisonment. Do not keep employees in an interview against their will. Avoid coercive tactics not only because of the law but because they are bad HR practice.

Chapter 3 Self-Check

This chapter has given you an overview of major legal concepts affecting investigations of workplace harassment. To further your knowledge, consider the following questions. Where applicable, answers have been provided in Appendix A. Other answers will depend on details particular to your organization.

1. What factors have courts looked to in order to determine whether an investigation was reasonable?
2. If an employee complains about harassment and the employer investigates and finds no that harassment took place, could the employee file a lawsuit?
3. Think back to the last investigation your organization did. Was it thorough? Were all necessary witnesses spoken to? Were you confident with the findings? What, if anything, could have been done to improve the investigation?

Investigations: When to Do Them, Who Should Do Them, and What to Investigate

Well-planned and well-enforced employer policies go far to prevent harassment in the workplace, but not all harassment can be prevented. Various forms of harassment occur in nearly every workplace. The key is to recognize problems early and respond promptly and appropriately. When a complaint of harassment is filed, or when a supervisor notices behavior that might be harassment, the organization must determine what occurred. Often it is impossible to collect sufficient relevant information to make a determination about an incident or complaint *without* conducting an investigation. Behavior that could be harassment generally requires an analysis of the context in which it occurred and an explanation of the interpretations placed on the statements, actions, or events by the participants and various witnesses. These variables can be difficult to understand without an investigation.

Figure 7 illustrates the typical decision-making cycle that begins with the employer's first awareness of a complaint or when a manager or HR specialist observes a situation that may be a violation of the organization's harassment-free workplace policy. Some of the items in Figure 7 will be discussed in the next several chapters.

Employers have a responsibility to conduct timely, fair, and thorough investigations of complaints of workplace harassment. The law dictates that employers must take "all necessary steps to prevent harassment from occurring." A demonstrated willingness to respond promptly to complaints supports the employer's prevention efforts and investigations can help an employer uncover and improve areas of weakness in its prevention policies and procedures.

An employer's response to a complaint, and specifically when and how an investigation was conducted, may be placed under great scruti-

Figure 7. A Typical Investigation

Information "triggers" that can launch an inquiry or an investigation of an alleged incident of workplace harassment may include
- anonymous communications (verbal or written);
- observations made by employees, supervisors, or managers;
- employee complaint; or
- receipt of a regulatory agency complaint.

An initial inquiry may be handled by
- a trained supervisor or manager;
- a trained security specialist;
- an HR representative;
- an EEO or affirmative action specialist; or even
- a trained senior staff member or executive.

An initial inquiry may
- suffice for the employer to determine what happened and implement appropriate remedial actions, if any are needed; or
- reveal information that causes the employer to begin a full investigation.

If a full investigation is needed, it should
- be handled by a neutral, experienced, and trained investigator, working alone or in a team;
- comply with and be supported by the employer's written policies covering harassment; and
- be supported by a senior staff that recognizes the mandate to set aside necessary resources, including staff time, to ensure a thorough, fair, and legal investigation.

While maintaining all necessary confidentiality, the investigator may be required to coordinate with outside entities that may include
- legal counsel;
- EEOC or other regulatory agency officials;
- union representatives;
- law enforcement personnel; and
- attorneys representing the complainant, respondent, or witnesses.

The investigation itself generally involves collecting and documenting information by conducting interviews with and obtaining signed statements from
- the complainant;
- the respondent;
- witnesses to the events, incidents, relationships pertinent to the complaint; and
- supervisors or managers who were responsible for knowing and enforcing organizational nonharassment policies.

Figure 7. *continued* A Typical Investigation

Additional interviews or research may be required to determine, among other details, any evidence of
- prior offensive behavior;
- behavior that extends beyond the initial complaint to involve additional offenses or other possible victims;
- complicating factors among the parties, such as friendships or dating relationships carried on outside the workplace; or
- complicating factors among the parties, such as work-related grudges.

The investigation usually concludes with development of a written report that
- documents the information gathered in the investigation;
- presents the findings of the investigation; and
- if requested, outlines the remedial measures or remedies (including any disciplinary actions) that the employer will take consistent with the employer's policies on workplace harassment.

The investigator may be instructed to prepare communications using guidelines that balance the need for confidentiality against the parties' legal rights and need to know to
- the complainant;
- the respondent;
- witnesses;
- the HR department (permanent and confidential files); and
- external legal, law enforcement, or judicial entities that may require copies pursuant to litigation.

Following submission of the report with the employer's findings, the supervisor or HR investigator
- implements and documents any required remedial and disciplinary actions ranging from counseling to termination, and
- facilitates the transition back to a normal working environment for all employees in the affected workgroups.

---

ny, especially if the problem is not resolved and ends up in court. Most people understand the importance of a fair and thorough investigation. Nonetheless, employees, managers, and even senior executives may ask many questions, such as

- Should the employer investigate every complaint of harassment?
- Should the employer conduct an investigation whenever a supervisor sees behavior that could be unwanted or offensive, even if no one has complained? What about a cartoon, a stray comment, or an anonymous letter?

- Can a supervisor look into any matter without involving the HR department? What are the criteria for when HR must become involved?
- Can supervisors ignore matters that they consider to be trivial?
- Who will do the investigation?
- What are the components of a fair and thorough investigation?
- What should be done in a "he said, she said" situation?

When Is an Investigation Necessary?

Many supervisors and employees balk at the idea that every incident of possible harassment must be investigated. Some complaints clearly relate to behavior that was unquestionably minor. In such cases, conducting an investigation may make a "mountain out of a molehill," dividing staff loyalties into camps and needlessly disrupting operations and using up company resources. Supervisors and managers also often fear that an investigation will open a "Pandora's box," prompting employees to air grievances and complaints that have already been dealt with or that are so trivial they would normally receive no attention. No one wants to see minor situations escalate or good employees hurt by rumors and innuendo. Yet possible harassment cannot be ignored. So what's an employer to do?

The answer is that the employer must attend to *all* possible harassment—the stray joke, the complaint from the flaky employee who complains about everything, the cartoon forwarded through e-mail, even the anonymous letter. But attending to every incident does not mean that every incident must receive a full investigation.

One option is to perform an "inquiry." An inquiry can help an organization determine whether a more in-depth investigation is necessary. Depending on what the inquiry reveals, it alone may be sufficient for an employer to say that a problem was "attended to." A full investigation probably is *not* necessary if a supervisor sees possible harassment that (according to the employer's stated policies) is not very serious or if a complainant alleges conduct that is relatively minor and the parties have admitted the conduct involved. In such situations, the supervisor may look into the situation or the HR department may conduct an inquiry to determine what else, if anything, needs to be done. It is recommended that HR be involved even if only an inquiry takes place. Remember, a supervisor may see something minor but be unaware of past conduct. It is HR's responsibility to track this information.

Here are some examples that illustrate factors that influence an employer's response to a complaint of harassment. (Note: These examples are not meant to demonstrate the discipline an employer should take in any given situation. Disciplinary action is covered in Chapter 10.)

Example #4

Dorothy, Judy, and the Racial Joke

Dorothy, a supervisor, is forwarded an e-mail that contains a racial joke. She determines that Judy, a worker in her unit, originated the e-mail by bringing in and scanning a document. Dorothy notices that Judy sent the e-mail to several co-workers in her unit and that some of the co-workers have forwarded it on to a number of other employees. No one has reported being offended by the e-mail. Dorothy contacts HR and is informed that no prior complaints or incidents of a similar nature have been reported. HR gives Dorothy the authority to handle the situation on her own, and informs her to report back as to what action she took.

Dorothy decides to talk privately to Judy about the company's policy regarding harassment and about what would generally be considered unprofessional and inappropriate conduct relative to e-mail. When Dorothy speaks with Judy, Judy readily admits that she has forwarded e-mails. Dorothy then brings up the topic at a meeting with all employees, without mentioning any names. The group has a discussion about the company policies regarding e-mail and harassment and after the discussion Dorothy believes that everyone in the unit has gained a better understanding. Dorothy informs HR of her actions and a note about what occurred is placed in Judy's personnel file. Dorothy continues to monitor the work environment to prevent any other or future problems. Is any other action needed?

In this situation additional action probably is not necessary. The inappropriate e-mail appears to be an isolated incident. Dorothy has made a reasonable inquiry into the incident by checking Judy's personnel file. The incident appears not to be serious—no employee has complained of being offended and the e-mail is not aimed at or intended to demean anyone specifically. Dorothy has let Judy know that she made a mistake and educated her about why. She also has let the workgroup know her expectations about the appropriate and inappropriate use of e-mail relative to the organization's harassment-free workplace policy. The problem has been handled and a full investigation is not necessary.

Assume that when Dorothy is looking into the e-mail situation with Judy, she discovers e-mails with racial comments about specific employees. Now further action should be taken. This situation warrants an investigation. Because the comments have been directed at specific targets, the employer will want to interview those people to determine if anything had been said to them directly and to investigate whether other offensive conduct may have occurred or if the e-mails have had other effects on the targeted employees. More serious disciplinary action also should be taken because conduct aimed at specific employees is far more hurtful and damaging than generic comments. Thus Dorothy would contact HR and an investigator would be assigned.

Example #5

Charlie and Linda

Charlie complains to his supervisor, Allen, that one day when he was alone with his co-worker, Linda, she touched his arm and told him he was a very attractive man—maybe they should go out sometime. Charlie felt uncomfortable and didn't know how to tell Linda to stop. He says he is now afraid to be alone with Linda. He says this is the only time Linda has made him feel uncomfortable and he is unaware of Linda "bothering" anyone else.

Allen talks to Linda about the incident. Linda admits that it happened. She says she thought Charlie liked her, but perhaps she misread the signals. Linda says she realized she was wrong when it happened and she is embarrassed about the situation. She promises that it won't happen again. Allen gives Linda an oral warning and documents the warning by placing a note in Linda's personnel file. He then goes to Charlie and tells him Linda knows she was wrong and has said it won't happen again. Allen checks to be sure Charlie is comfortable with this solution and assures Charlie that he can come to Allen if there are future problems. Charlie tells Allen that he considers the matter closed.

In this situation an investigation is not necessary. Allen has not ignored Charlie's complaint and he has taken appropriate actions in response to it. Some employers might take more formal disciplinary actions against Linda—but Charlie's statement that he considers the matter closed is a good indication that he is comfortable with the actions Allen has taken.

Now assume that Linda is Charlie's supervisor or a supervisor in another department. Linda's status as a supervisor will affect the disciplinary action taken. Her behavior automatically is considered to be more serious because it has come from a supervisor. Linda's status as a supervisor will not affect the decision to investigate. Because Linda has admitted to the behavior—and the employer feels confident that the offensive action was limited to a single incident—an investigation is not needed.

Now assume that when Allen talks to Linda she denies the incident and says that Charlie is making it up to get her in trouble because Charlie wanted to go out with her but she refused.

In this situation an investigation is necessary to determine if the acts Charlie has alleged did occur. If they did occur, disciplinary action must be taken against Linda. If they did not occur, it would be unfair to discipline her. Indeed, if the investigation reveals that Charlie has falsely accused Linda, it might be appropriate to discipline Charlie.

Example #6

Marta and Carl

Marta complains that her supervisor, Carl, made an inappropriate comment. Marta states that she was trying to file something but the drawer was stuck and she said out loud, "I'm having a hard time getting into this drawer." She states that Carl then said, "I'd like to get into your drawers." She tells you that nothing else inappropriate has been done or said by Carl, though she has never felt comfortable around him. Carl's record shows no prior complaints and Marta knows of no one else who has been bothered by him. Carl denies having said anything at all. He has no recollection of Marta complaining about the file drawer and he says the comment is not the type of thing he would say.

Here, even though Carl has denied the incident, it appears that further investigation would not be fruitful. If the conduct were serious—such as unwanted touching—an investigation would be called for. But in this situation even if Carl made the comment, it could have been innocently made and simply misinterpreted. Therefore even a finding that the comment occurred would not necessarily lead to disciplinary action. Reminding both employees of policies against harassment, coupled with monitoring of the situation, is sufficient remedial action in this case. Of course, the complaint and the inquiry should be documented. Assistance with the working relationship between Marta and Carl also might be in order. But an investigation would be neither necessary nor helpful.

Is It Ever Appropriate Not to Investigate?

In rare situations, an employer may decide it is not necessary to conduct a full investigation even when the offending behavior has been denied. Such decisions may be appropriate, but they should be approached with caution.

Many employers make the mistake of not investigating disputed situations that have no third-party witnesses. These employers think they will never uncover the truth—it is a hopeless "he said, she said" situation. But failing to investigate and make a determination is a mistake. As will be discussed later, credibility determinations must and can be made even when there are no independent witnesses.

Managers, and some HR representatives, may be tempted to discount complaints received by poor-performing employees, chronic complainers, or individuals who have recently been disciplined. Human beings naturally tend to "consider the source" when we know of a history of conflict relating to a person. With respect to harassment or discrimination complaints, however, we should avoid the temptation to minimize any harassment complaint because of the past experience or reputation of the complainant. In some cases the poor performance may be a result of the harassment and the disciplinary action is the incentive to complain. Be careful not to assume anything.

It is far better to err on the side of investigating something that does not need to be investigated than to fail to investigate something when you should have. Treat every complaint as equally valid. The inquiry or investigation will give you the opportunity to examine the complainant's sincerity. Although your concerns about a complainant may prove to be valid, they also could prevent you from investigating a legitimate complaint. The specific circumstances of each complaint will help you determine whether an investigation is needed. A summary of the main criteria for when you must investigate appears in Figure 8.

Investigating the Anonymous Complaint

An employer may become aware of harassment through an anonymous letter or a rumor that harassment is taking place. An employer's responsibility for responding to potential harassment does not go away simply because there is no way of identifying who complained. A reasonable investigation must take place. The investigation will vary depending on the allegations, and executing this type of investigation takes some ingenuity.

Figure 8. When to Investigate

You must do an investigation when

■ the facts conflict and the conduct is more than trivial;

■ you discover any indication of questionable conduct that has not yet surfaced, such as rumors about an individual or a manager's instinct that the problems run deeper than what is seen from the surface;*

■ a manager is implicated in potential harassment by his or her subordinates.

An investigation may not be necessary when

■ the offensive conduct is admitted by the respondent—as long as you have uncovered all of the behavior; or

■ the conduct is denied, there were no witnesses, and the conduct itself was not serious, such as an isolated comment that could be taken two different ways.

■ When in doubt, investigate!

*Rumors are information. They should not be considered reliable information until they have been corroborated—but they should not be ignored.

To investigate such a complaint you probably will have to start with interviewing employees generally about the work environment. One approach is to use survey-type questions about the general features of the work environment in relation to informality, racial or ethnic joking, sexually explicit content, and the like. Where you start and how you proceed will depend on what clues you have been given in the letter or rumors. Some examples of survey-type questions are

■ How would you describe the work environment in regard to how formal it is? Why?

■ Do people play practical jokes on each other? What sort of jokes?

■ How often have you heard a joke that involves a reference to sexual activity, race, or ethnicity?

■ If you have heard jokes, are they usually initiated by the same person or people?

By asking general questions in a manner that does not suggest you are making a judgment, you may be able to uncover the circumstances that gave rise to an anonymous complaint.

Investigating Harassment from Anonymous Sources

Harassment may take the form of anonymous letters or other written communication directed to a specific individual. The recipients of such items usually respond with a mixture of emotions, including shock, anger, and self-blame. The human resources department and managers learn of the communications but, because they are anonymously authored, it is hard to know what, if anything, can be done. As with anonymous complaints, anonymous harassment should not be ignored. The employer's obligation to protect employees from harassment extends to all forms of harassment that are offensive and unwelcome to complainants, including anonymous written communication. In serious cases the use of handwriting or voice recognition experts may be necessary. On rare occasions an employer may use surveillance to assist in determining the source of harassment. For example, surveillance might include security cameras positioned in an area where racial epithets have been written. Privacy rights must be taken into account when surveillance is considered. Employers are advised to get legal advice before embarking on the use of surveillance.

When an anonymous letter has offended an employee, consider taking one or more of the following investigative steps.

- Discuss the letter privately with the recipient. Attempt to learn who the recipient believes may have sent or handled the letter before he or she received it. Ask the recipient about work relationships that may have changed recently.
- Examine the document closely for any potential clues about the author, the relationship between the author and the recipient, and any expectation the author might have for some kind of a response.
- Check the details of how the recipient received the communication. Did anyone else observe anything about the place or time when the communication was delivered?
- If the recipient believes that he or she knows one or more potential sources for the communication, interview those individuals. Use an indirect line of questioning and do not show the communication unless you strongly suspect you are interviewing the author. (For information about indirect questions, see Chapter 8.)
- If the method of delivering the communication was electronic, check the availability of backup or archiving system software on the office network. Make sure that technical support staffers know to be discreet

and to maintain strict confidentiality regarding your inquiry and the people involved.

■ If you are unable to determine the source of the communication, continue to monitor the workplace in an attempt to assure that the behavior is not repeated.

Example #7

Mary and the Graffiti

Mary is the only female employee on a construction crew. She shares a portable latrine with the men. She is offended by the graffiti that has appeared in the latrine and that is hateful toward women. She becomes outraged when the latrine begins to contain demeaning graffiti specifically aimed at her. The employer's solution is to provide Mary with her own latrine. She has to walk a long distance (past the men's latrine and sometimes in the rain) to get to it. This latrine also becomes covered with graffiti and is further defaced with urine and feces. The employer can't understand why Mary keeps complaining. No one knows who is responsible for the graffiti. What can the employer do?

Unfortunately the employer hasn't asked Mary what else can be done. She might say, "Paint over the graffiti, tell the employees why the harassing behavior is wrong, and—if it continues—provide surveillance." These solutions might be costly, but they would cost the employer far less than dealing with a lawsuit. In a case based on similar circumstances, the complainant did file a lawsuit, which ultimately was settled for both money and a change in the employer's policies.

Who Should Investigate?

The person who investigates a complaint of harassment should be a neutral party, have the requisite amount of experience, and be comfortable doing the investigation. When an inquiry has established enough facts to warrant an investigation, HR and the employer's legal counsel may become involved in selecting the proper person to investigate. When HR cannot assign someone to investigate—because, for example, an HR person is involved in the complaint—the company's executives will make the decision, often with the assistance of legal counsel.

Biases and Ignorance

Because an investigator is vulnerable to charges of being biased, he or she must take care that no action or statement he or she makes should appear to betray personal judgments. An investigator who is seen to favor the complainant runs the risk of losing the respondent's cooperation. On the other hand, investigators who believe they serve the employer's best interest by helping the employer "avoid liability" may be tempted to make flawed or erroneous findings that harassment did not occur or was not very serious. When a biased investigator allows his or her investigation to go forward, the employer may take the wrong action, resulting in increased liability. Furthermore, when the investigation is closely examined, the investigator's bias usually becomes obvious.

Investigators must serve only the truth. They must work to uncover the truth regardless of where the investigation leads. Factors that can interfere with a fair and thorough investigation include

- organizational reporting relationships or alliances that prevent neutrality;
- an investigator's unrecognized biases about harassment in the workplace, such as "men can't be harassed," "women don't harass women," "visual harassment isn't very serious," "members of racial minority groups do not demean members of another minority," "Latinos tend to verbally harass women," and so on;
- an investigator's preconceived ideas about what harassment "looks like," such as "only unwanted touching can be harassment," or "if someone is feeling harassed he or she would say something";
- an investigator's previous knowledge about one or more of the parties or witnesses that affects how he or she views the facts; and
- an investigator's fear of having to fire someone—particularly if the investigation reveals that the conduct occurred.

No human being is free of all biases. Furthermore, an investigator may have previous experience with the parties to a complaint and still behave in a neutral way. The important thing is to recognize the issues and how they may influence your thinking. Being able to recognize your own biases and the barriers they create to conducting a neutral investigation can help you overcome them. The investigator must determine if he or she can be neutral given the particulars of any investigation.

Example #8

Sharon's Misgivings

Sharon, who is African American, has been asked to investigate a complaint of racial harassment against Julio. When Julio was first hired, Sharon noticed that during the orientation she led he wouldn't look at her or ask her questions but instead asked Maryanne, a Caucasian trainee from HR who was observing the orientation. Sharon has had little contact with Julio since the orientation. She thinks that Julio may be a racist. Should Sharon investigate the complaint?

The answer to this question depends on whether Sharon is confident that she can put her own feelings aside. She has little objective basis for believing that Julio is a racist. If her residual feelings about Julio will make her tend to believe the complainant and to disbelieve Julio, she should ask not to be assigned to investigate this complaint. If she feels certain that Julio's failure to engage with her during the orientation and his questioning of Maryanne, rather than her, was racially based, she might ask that someone else do the investigation. Sharon can then offer herself as a possible witness to prior acts that could be evidence of racial bias.

Example #9

Stuart and the Chronic Complainer

Al has filed a complaint of racial harassment against Agnes, which Stuart has been asked to investigate. Al has filed complaints before that proved to be unfounded, and Stuart has heard about them. Stuart has no opinion as to whether this complaint is legitimate. Should he investigate?

If Stuart truly has no opinion about this complaint, there is no reason for him not to investigate. He will learn more about the other complaints in the course of this investigation, and he will need to weigh the relevance of these other complaints. But knowing about them before he begins this investigation will not necessarily create an unfair bias.

Biases often play a large role in our thinking about people, especially people who appear to be different from us in some way. Sometimes an individual's biases or misunderstandings about a certain group can interfere with his or her ability to conduct a neutral investigation. The more you can recognize your own biases and the more you are willing to educate yourself about people who are different from you, the less those biases will interfere with your ability to be fair.

Example #10

Marsha's Assumptions

Kenneth, an openly gay clerical employee, is not shy about talking about his boyfriend and the places they go on the weekends (ski trips, movies, and so forth). On his birthday, Kenneth's co-worker publicly presents him with a gag gift that is explicitly sexual. Kenneth is mortified and complains to his supervisor, Marsha. Marsha can't understand why Kenneth has complained—she feels that he initiated talking about sex in the workplace by telling everyone he is gay and has a boyfriend. Marsha wonders, what does he expect? Is Marsha's reaction understandable?

Marsha's reaction is a common one, but it is nonetheless biased. A common misconception about gays is that when they talk about their relationships, they are talking about sex. When Kenneth discusses things like going to the movies with his boyfriend, he is no more talking about sex than Marsha is when she mentions going to the movies with her husband. But Marsha believes that talking about a gay relationship is the same as talking about sex—so she is unable to see why the gag joke is inappropriate.

Marsha may not be an appropriate person to investigate Kenneth's complaint. Marsha's unrecognized bias seems to prevent her from understanding the facts from Kenneth's perspective. If Marsha is unable to understand Kenneth's perspective, her bias may be clear to him—and he may conclude that she doesn't take his complaint seriously.

But whether Marsha's biased thoughts alone should prevent her from investigating is not so simple. Thoughts must be distinguished from conduct. Everyone has thoughts and ideas that exhibit bias, but these thoughts do not always result in discriminatory conduct. If Marsha is aware of her biases and is willing to reexamine them in light of Kenneth's thoughts and feelings, she might be qualified to do a fair and neutral investigation.

It is incumbent on every investigator to examine his or her biases and make a fair determination as to whether he or she can be neutral. Some Jewish people could never impartially investigate a complaint against a member of the Nazi party, and some African Americans could never impartially investigate a complaint against a member of the Ku Klux

Klan. Yet there also are Jewish people and African Americans who could be unbiased in such investigations. Who you are does not determine your ability to be neutral—rather, it is your ability to put aside whatever biases you may have about a particular group or behavior in order to make a determination in light of the facts presented.

Neutrality and the Appearance of Neutrality

Investigators may in fact be neutral yet may not appear neutral to others. In such situations, the organization's leadership should think carefully about who should investigate the complaint, particularly if it is a serious complaint.

Example #11

Joan's Reporting Relationship

Carlos has lodged a complaint of national origin harassment against Philippe, the number-two person in the company. Joan, a seasoned investigator, reports to Philippe on some issues and directly to the company CEO on other issues. Philippe has input on Joan's performance review. Despite the reporting relationship, Joan believes she can be neutral in conducting the investigation. She has been with the company longer than Philippe and has a good relationship with the CEO. Should Joan be the investigator?

In this situation despite Joan's experience and the fact that she may indeed be able to conduct the investigation in a neutral manner, she should not investigate the complaint. If Carlos is unhappy with the results—and there's a fifty-fifty chance that he will be—Carlos can call the entire investigation into question based on the strong appearance of bias due to Joan's reporting relationship to Philippe.

Experience and Comfort Level

The investigator should be knowledgeable about workplace harassment and have experience and training in how to conduct an investigation. The more serious the allegations, the more experience the investigator should have. Similarly, the higher up the chain of command the parties are, the more experience the investigator should have. Generally the investigation suffers if the investigator has less authority in the organization than the person who is the subject of the investigation. No fixed formula determines at what point an investigator has the requisite knowledge and experience. The investigator, however, should feel comfortable with his or her level of experience given the allegations and issues presented. In cases involving serious allegations, the investigator should be someone who would be comfortable if he or she had to testify in court.

Example #12

Molly's Discomfort

Molly has the unfortunate job of investigating a complaint alleging that Sam was masturbating while at work. Molly is embarrassed about having to discuss the details of some of the allegations. When she questions Sam, she does not feel comfortable asking him specific questions about what he did—doing so seems much too personal and invasive. Should Molly have agreed to investigate this complaint?

Molly should not be the person assigned to do this investigation. Her difficulty in interviewing Sam shows the importance of an investigator knowing herself and her limits. Doing an investigation often means asking embarrassing questions and repeating words and phrases that are repugnant to many people. If an investigator will feel uncomfortable with questioning witnesses about the allegations, he or she should say so before agreeing to embark on the investigation. On the one hand, it is not advisable for organizational leaders to put an investigator in a position that will make him or her uncomfortable. On the other hand, a thorough investigation often cannot be accomplished without asking some tough questions. When an investigator senses that he or she cannot pursue tough but necessary questions, it is very important that the investigator consult with a manager or legal counsel and discuss the source of the discomfort. Organizational leaders (and, if necessary, legal counsel) can then determine whether the investigator should be replaced or if he or she can, with some coaching, proceed.

Organizational Hierarchy Designations

Organizational levels constitute an important lens through which an investigation of workplace harassment must be sighted. Harassment often involves a power difference between the complainant and the respondent. A thorough investigator will anticipate this power difference and plan to include investigative queries that reveal the power relationships between and among the various parties to the complaint, including the witnesses. To succeed using such an approach, the investigator must have sufficient stature within the organization to avoid intimidation as he or she proceeds with the investigation.

A well-planned investigation attends to the question of reporting relationships involving the investigator and the complainant, respondent, and important witnesses. The investigator should not have a direct reporting relationship to the complainant or respondent. If a reporting relationship has existed between the investigator and witnesses, arrangements for a temporary change of reporting relationships should be made. Investigators must be free to follow leads, interview witnesses, and determine findings without fear of repercussions to them or their career aspirations with the organization.

A Team Approach

One way an HR department can minimize questions about neutrality and organizational rank is to use two investigators in a team. The team approach provides a new investigator with valuable guidance while he or she gains experience and offers the employer many other advantages. A team benefits by using two sets of ears and eyes. One investigator may think of questions the other investigator would not have thought of. One investigator can ask questions while the other investigator observes closely, possibly noticing clues that would have eluded someone working alone. Even experienced investigators can benefit from working in a team.

Employers can balance an investigative team to suit the context of the investigation. Thus, in a sexual harassment case, the employer might assign a male-female team or in a race-based harassment case the team might include members that represent the races of the complainant and respondent. Balancing team members this way may engender more trust from the parties because both sides will see that their perspective is represented. Of course, people do not always think or feel along gender or race lines. Yet having this balance may reassure complainants, respondents, or witnesses about the essential fairness of the investigation.

Team investigations also present challenges. It may be difficult to keep witness information coordinated among two or more investigators. This difficulty can occur if the investigators are not always together during the information-gathering phase of the investigation. Tensions can develop if team members disagree about the course of the investigation.

When a team investigation would be advisable but it is not possible for you to work with a partner, consider establishing a connection with someone else within the organization that you can trust—such as an HR colleague—to talk about the investigation as it proceeds. As you evaluate the information you receive, you may find it helpful to solicit this person's reactions. To preserve confidentiality, however, limit the number of people with whom you discuss the investigation to the necessary few: the participants in the investigation, your supervisor, and your trusted advisor.

Executives as Investigators

When a top executive will act as the investigator, the HR department must consider the impact that such a selection will have on the workforce. Employees who would otherwise admit problems, or perhaps admit to a certain amount of looseness in their conduct, may be unwilling to do so when questioned by an authority who controls their evaluations and promotion opportunities. This consideration does not mean that a top executive should not do an investigation—assuming that he or she has the skills, the available time, and is the most appropriate person to do the investigation. Nonetheless, part of doing a good investigation is putting people at ease so that they feel comfortable being honest and open. HR needs to make sure that whoever will conduct the investigation will be able to talk with the various parties and obtain the necessary information.

Situations do occur when the top executive will be the appropriate investigator. For example, in one small and geographically remote division of a large corporation, a new unit manager learned of an uninvestigated, pre-existing racial harassment complaint involving two co-workers. Because the unit manager had training and experience in investigations and because she didn't know any of the witnesses, the organization correctly determined that she was the right person to investigate the complaint and report her findings to HR.

Lawyers as Investigators

Many employers think that using a lawyer as an investigator will help protect the company against potential legal liability. In some cases this may be true. A lawyer with the proper expertise may anticipate and deal with issues during the course of a harassment investigation that a less knowledgeable individual would miss. Some employers wrongly believe that using an attorney will keep the investigation confidential if a lawsuit is filed. If your company elects to use an attorney to conduct an investigation, some cautions are in order.

■ Not all lawyers have suitable experience or interpersonal communication skills to be investigators.

■ The attorney-client privilege probably will not be upheld if the company defends a lawsuit based on the fact that it did a fair investigation. Therefore, in trial, the company will have to choose between keeping the investigation confidential or using it as a defense in the lawsuit.

■ The investigator may need to testify in court. Therefore, the lawyer doing the investigation probably will not be able to represent the company in litigation.

Companies should make sure that they are willing to accept these considerations before retaining a lawyer to conduct a harassment investigation. Note that hiring an investigator who is also a lawyer but who will not function as the company's lawyer is a far different choice from hiring a lawyer whom you expect to both represent the company and to investigate. It is the latter situation that can lead to problems.

Internal and External Investigators

One decision that the company will need to make is whether the investigator should be an employee—an internal investigator—or someone from the outside. Figure 9 summarizes some of the advantages and disadvantages of using an investigator from outside the organization. Whether an employer uses an internal or an external investigator will depend, in part, on the resources within the company and the nature of the complaint. Does the employer have a trained and experienced investigator who can begin work right away? How serious is the complaint? Against whom has it been filed? Does the employer know how to retain a qualified external investigator? Some states require outside investigators who are not attorneys to be licensed private investigators.

Some harassment complaints will need to be investigated by a person from outside the organization. The most obvious situations involve complaints against the highest-level manager in the organization. An outside investigator may also be preferable if there is a serious complaint against

---

Figure 9. Advantages and Disadvantages of Using an Outside Investigator

Advantages	Disadvantages
Usually appears more neutral	Costs more
Usually has more experience	Usually takes longer
Is comfortable testifying if necessary	Doesn't know organizational culture
Comes to the situation with no preconceived ideas about the individuals involved	May have obligations under the FCRA to disclose the report
Doesn't take employees' time away from other work	

---

a high-ranking individual. If a complaint is likely to go to litigation, the employer should contact the company's attorney as early as possible and consider whether to bring in an outside investigator.

In some situations potential internal investigators from the organization's HR department may have problematic prior experiences with employees. HR employees may be perceived as biased because of past experiences with these individuals (or employees' perceptions of past events). In some cases victims of harassment may find it hard to believe that any HR person who has previously been viewed as an arm of the organization's leadership will take their allegations seriously. Employers should take these concerns into consideration when deciding who should investigate.

An external investigation should be free of even the appearance of interference by an employer and its outside counsel. In an adversarial proceeding, the independence of the investigator would be an important topic of contention. The best practice is for an external investigator to be given, in writing, a "free hand" in all matters necessary to the conduct of an unbiased, fair, and thorough investigation.

An external investigator needs a designated "internal contact" within the employer's organization to assist with routine matters such as scheduling meeting rooms and making copies of confidential documents. The internal contact should not otherwise be involved in the investigation (e.g. as a witness) and should be trustworthy in handling private information.

External Investigators and the Fair Credit Reporting Act

In 1999 a Federal Trade Commission opinion stated that the federal Fair Credit Reporting Act (FCRA) applied to investigations of harassment conducted by external investigators. The FCRA requirement entailed disclosures that hindered the investigations and led to problems with confidentiality. In 2003, the FCRA was amended. Current law requires only that if an outside investigator is used and if the investigation results in adverse action, the accused receive a summary of the "nature and substance" of the investigator's report. The law expressly permits nondisclosure of witnesses' identities.

Determining Supervisors' and Managers' Roles

Many investigations will need to include questions about supervisor or manager involvement in or awareness of harassment situations. An investigator may become concerned that supervisors' previous responses to harassment claims have been inadequate or that a given supervisor responded inappropriately to knowledge of harassment.

An employer may elect to investigate supervisors' and managers' knowledge of and response to harassment claims separately, or include this aspect in the investigation but separate it from other issues in the formal written report. Investigating the knowledge and actions of management provides the employer with information about how well managers and supervisors understand the policies against harassment. It also gives the employer a better understanding of potential legal liability and an opportunity to correct problems.

In your investigations be sure to ask witnesses about whether they ever complained to a supervisor or manager and if so, how the complaint was handled; whether they believe supervisors were aware of behavior and if so, why, and so forth. Witnesses who are supervisors should be queried about their understanding of company policies and the procedures for reporting complaints. A supervisor who had some involvement in a complaint should be questioned about what he or she did and why. The goal is to obtain information about the employer's response to the harassment when it first surfaced.

Special Situations

Sometimes an employer's response to harassment must reflect and accommodate the influences of external agencies. Such situations include cases when a claim already has been filed with an administrative agency or when a claim involves a charge of criminal conduct.

Action Filed with an Administrative Agency

Some companies fail to investigate when the complainant has filed an action with the EEOC or state fair employment agency. These employers wrongly think that once another investigation has begun, theirs can (or should) end. In some cases, the employer first receives notice of the complaint when administrative charges are filed and concludes, again wrongly, that the matter is now in the agency's hands. An employer's duty to investigate does not stop because a complaint has been filed with an administrative agency. Moreover, agency investigations are notoriously slow. The employer must make its own determination as to what occurred and what action to take, regardless of what the agency does.

Of course, when a complaint is filed with an administrative agency, the employer will need to respond to the agency. The employer's response may include interviews with witnesses and documentation. Although employers may be tempted to consider that response an "investigation," the response an employer puts together for a government agency is unlikely to be as impartial and thorough as the type of investigation described in this book. The employer is defending its actions—not really examining them. Therefore, an employer's response to an agency about a harassment claim generally will be an inadequate substitute for an investigation.

Example #13

An Employer's Response to the EEOC

An employer receives a complaint from the EEOC alleging that Emily, while an employee, experienced racial harassment from Fred, a co-worker, and that afterward, Emily quit. The employer checks with Emily's manager, Fred's manager, and the HR person who did the exit interview. All three sources say that although Emily had complained to HR six months before she quit, the problem was determined to be a minor personality dispute that had been resolved and Emily ultimately quit because she was planning to return to school. The employer does not interview

Emily, Fred, or other potential witnesses. The employer informs the EEOC that no harassment took place.

This employer's response to the EEOC does not meet the criteria for an adequate investigation. Without an independent investigation a potential harasser (Fred) could continue to be employed without appropriate disciplinary and remedial action being taken. When Emily's complaint resurfaces by way of the EEOC complaint, the employer should go back and take another look at the situation. The employer should make its own determination as to whether Fred violated the employer's rules and, depending on the specific allegations, whether Fred has harassed anyone else. Whether this employer's response to the EEOC was adequate is beyond the purview of this book. The issue here is that the complaint was never really investigated by the employer and that the employer should not now wait for the EEOC to investigate. Given the EEOC's backlog, the EEOC investigation will probably not be timely. Also, the EEOC will apply a different standard than would the employer. The EEOC will find cause only if the law has been violated. As was discussed earlier, the employer's policies may have been violated even if the law has not been. For all these reasons, the employer should do its own investigation.

Police Involvement

Some acts of harassment constitute criminal assault. A victim of serious harassment may want to speak with the police or district attorney about criminal charges. In such cases employers should cooperate with the complainant's decision. In some situations that involve serious charges—rape, sexual assault, and situations involving minors—and situations that would be difficult for the company to investigate, an employer may want to contact the police on behalf of the complainant or assist the complainant with contacting the police. The police can use investigative techniques that generally are not available to an employer. For example, except in very limited circumstances, a private employer violates the Employee Polygraph Protection Act if it forces an employee to take a lie detector test. The police also have ready access to criminal background information.

Police involvement does not mean that the employer should stop its own investigation. The criteria for establishing criminal liability are very different from what is necessary to establish if an employer's policy has been violated. Again, the employer's duty to investigate and take action does not stop because another investigation is taking place. It is appropriate for an employer to share information with the police and vice versa.

Example #14

Sexual Assault of a Minor

Dianna, a seventeen-year-old server in a resort, is sitting in the break room when Albert puts his arm around her shoulder and touches her breast with his hand. Dianna runs out of the building. She returns to quit the next day, accompanied by her mother. The food and beverage manager meets with Dianna and her mother but can not persuade them to make a formal complaint. After listening to Dianna's account of what Albert did, the food and beverage manager telephones the local police. The food and beverage manager continues investigating the complaint.

The food and beverage manager is right to involve the police in this complaint because Dianna is a minor and because she is claiming that a sexual assault has occurred. Were Dianna not a minor, the decision of whether to involve the police would properly be left up to her, as the employee.

Chapter 4 Self-Check

This chapter has presented information that will help you define the scope of an investigation and who may take part in an investigation of workplace harassment. To further your knowledge, consider the following questions. Where applicable, answers have been provided in Appendix A. Other answers will depend on details particular to your organization.

1. It is likely that, if you have worked in HR or EEO for your organization for an extended time, some past experience(s) with an employee will challenge your ability to be neutral should that employee appear as a complainant or respondent in an investigation. Keep in mind that the challenge could be either that you might be too critical of that person or too uncritical. What steps could you take to try to maintain your neutrality should an occasion like this arise?

2. Assume that you are asked to investigate a complaint involving allegations about the behavior of top executives in your organization. Do you think you would be suitable to do this? If not, why not? How can you overcome those concerns?"

3. Who among your peers would be good for you to pair up with as part of an investigative team? Why did you select the person you did?

CHAPTER 5

Planning the Investigation

Spending a little time planning the investigation will help you anticipate and avoid problems that may crop up while the investigation is under way. The planning process need not be a lengthy one—you want to start the investigation as soon as possible. But thinking out issues such as who will be involved and where interviews will take place are crucial steps that should not be overlooked.

Once the employer has determined who the investigator will be, that investigator will need to get to work quickly. If you will be the investigator, a little advance planning will go a long way toward ensuring that the investigation is fair, thorough, and legal—and that it gathers the necessary information. As you plan the investigation, consider

- what adjustments to work assignments will be necessary during the investigation;
- how soon the investigation can begin and the best way to schedule interviews;
- where interviews can be conducted (give consideration to confidentiality);
- who must be interviewed (complainant, respondent, witnesses);
- participation in the investigation by any other parties;
- who has a need to know updated information as the information progresses;
- what documents and resources you will give to the complainant, respondent, and witnesses; and
- what documents or other evidence you will want to collect from the complainant, respondent, or from the workspace.

A checklist for planning the investigation is found at Figure 10.

Figure 10. Planning Checklist

- Make a list of issues and possible witnesses.
- Know which witnesses you will start with.
- Make a list of potential questions and anticipate difficult issues.
- Have all possible and available documents in your possession.
- Reserve a private place to conduct the interviews.
- Determine whom you will inform about the investigation and its progress.
- Know your organization's policy against harassment and have a copy of the written policy on hand.
- Know to what resources your organization can refer employees who need counseling or other services.
- Evaluate and decide whether the complainant, respondent, or both should be placed on leave or otherwise have a schedule change.
- Set aside the time you will need to focus on the investigation.

Work Assignments

If you are selected to do the investigation, you probably will need to be relieved from some or all of your regular duties in order to dedicate the necessary time and attention to the investigation. You also may need to enlist the cooperation of supervisors or managers in temporarily adjusting work assignments for the complainant, respondent, and witnesses.

You also will want to determine if it will be necessary to keep people separated during the investigation. The reason for keeping parties separate is to avoid further harm that ongoing contact between the parties might bring about and to avoid any opportunity for the person being investigated to disrupt the investigation. When the respondent is in a position of authority, his or her presence in the workplace during the investigation can intimidate witnesses. In this situation, particularly if the allegations are serious, the individual who has been accused typically is placed on paid administrative leave pending the outcome of the investigation. Other options include moving the respondent to another workspace, or having him or her work at home.

The determination to place a respondent on administrative leave may depend in part on whether there has been any threat of violence. If the respondent has made threats or has a history of violence (including unwanted physical touching), the respondent should be removed from the workplace until a determination is made either that there is no basis for the complainant to fear further harassment from the respondent or until the investigation is complete. When the complainant says he or she fears violence, but there have been no threats or violent acts, the employer will have to evaluate the situation and may want to call on an expert, such as an Employee Assistance Program (EAP) counselor, to assist in determining whether the complainant's fear is realistic under the circumstances.

Some employers make the mistake of moving the person who complained. Doing this can be seen as retaliation for making a complaint. Under the law, the person who complains should not suffer any adverse employment actions as a result of complaining. Occasionally, the complainant will ask to take time off or to transfer. If this happens, before taking such action, the employer must be very certain that the time off or the move is truly voluntary and desired by the complainant. The employer also should take care to be sure that the pay status for the complainant's time off work is worked out in a fashion that is acceptable to both the employer and the complainant and that the arrangement is documented.

It is a good idea to suspend any disciplinary actions toward parties and witnesses while the investigation is in progress. Employees who violate rules can be advised of unacceptable work behavior. But to avoid charges of retaliation, refrain from selecting or imposing discipline until the investigation is complete.

Timeliness

One hallmark of a good investigation is *timeliness*. Begin the investigation immediately, unless unusual circumstances—such as unchangeable vacation schedules of the complainant or respondent—make doing so impossible.

The investigator's vacation schedule should not dictate the timing of the investigation. If, for any reason, you are unavailable to start right away, usually it is best to step aside and allow the investigation to proceed with another investigator. The more serious the charges, the more urgent it is that the investigation begin immediately. This is one of the differences between investigating harassment (which implies the potential for ongoing abusive conduct) and investigating other forms of discrimination. For example, a discrimination complaint based on unequal pay does not have the same type of urgency as a harassment complaint because the primary damage to the complainant is financial rather than emotional.

Privacy

As you plan the investigation, consider where the interviews will take place. Because of the sensitive nature of a harassment investigation, the interviews need to take place in a private setting. You will need to arrange for an office space, if possible, in a location where whom you are questioning will not be obvious to the workgroup involved. The investigator's office or a conference room in HR usually are good places to conduct interviews. Plan not to take phone calls during interviews.

It is important to approach an investigation with due regard for the privacy of everyone, including the respondent. Even if the evidence later clears the respondent, there is a stigma attached to being the subject of a harassment complaint.

Witnesses sometimes express a preference for meeting with the investigator offsite. Generally it is acceptable to grant this request provided you can agree on a location that offers minimal distractions and provides the necessary level of privacy.

Making witnesses as comfortable as possible under the circumstances is a worthwhile goal. For example, an investigator can make sure there are facial tissues in the room and have water, coffee, and tea available.

Documents and Physical Evidence

Gather and review documents before you start. Include any written statements about the harassment (some employees keep diaries or there may be letters either from, to, or about the alleged harasser) and photographs or copies of any visual harassment, if applicable. You should look at the original document; however, you will not necessarily retain it. Most people like to hold on to their original documents. Making an accurate photocopy and returning the original to the party is acceptable practice. If you become aware of additional documents or physical evidence as the investigation progresses, you should obtain them. Also check personnel files to ascertain whether there have been past complaints of harassment and make a determination as to whether the earlier incidents are relevant to the current complaint.

Assemble copies of pertinent e-mails, cards, or letters. Store all physical and electronic evidence securely. You may need to consult with someone who has expertise in computer data storage in order to retrieve and store electronic communications. Evidence should be kept in a private (locked) location—this could be a file cabinet in your office or in HR. Use the same precautions as you would for confidential personnel information.

Telephone bills from work or home phones, cell phones, or pagers may provide corroboration of contact between the parties. The employer will be able to provide you with copies of bills from a work phone. If a home phone is involved, ask the parties to cooperate in providing copies.

Some investigations will involve physical evidence (such as pictures, gifts, and articles of clothing). Make every effort to ensure that important objects are preserved. If the owner of an object is unwilling to give it to you for safekeeping, photograph the object and keep the photographs in the investigation file.

Resources to Give the Parties

Assemble copies of the documents you will give the parties, including a copy of the company's harassment-free workplace policy and, in appropriate cases, referrals to counseling (EAP if available) and other contact numbers. If the employer has specified a procedure for a manager to make a referral to an EAP, authorize the investigator to activate the procedure without seeking additional approval.

Complaint Intake

Some organizations use specific forms and procedures to receive complaints of harassment. An intake form that is completed by a trained HR person can help assure consistency in the collection of information (see Figure 11). However, it is not a good idea to require that a complainant complete a form or give a written complaint before an investigation of his or her complaint commences. Such a requirement will intimidate some complainants and should not be imposed as a condition of starting an investigation. Also, an investigator who depends on the writing skill of a

---

Figure 11. Elements of an Intake Form

I. **General Information**
    This section of the form should include space and prompts to collect the
    following information.
    A. The complainant's name and contact information;
    B. The date of the complaint;
    C. The identity of the individual(s) who behaved inappropriately.

II. **Intake Interview**
    This section of the form should include space and prompts to collect the
    following information.
    A. The date of the intake interview;
    B. Any concerns the employee (complainant) may have expressed
        about possible problems that may arise investigating his or her
        complaint;
    C. Any documents or objects identified or referred to by the com-
        plainant that support the complaint:
    D. Any witnesses identified by the complainant, including details about
        the events or incidents allegedly witnessed; and
    E. Any other complaints or communications by the employee about
        the issue, and, if so, to whom they were made, and the results of
        raising the complaints.

---

complainant who fills out a form can expect to encounter difficulties later on in the investigation. An intake form can be a tool the employer uses
to help determine whether a complaint can be investigated by a simple
inquiry or requires a more in-depth investigation.

The intake form should be marked "Private and Confidential" and
should be maintained in a secure area consistent with the organization's
practices for handling and storing highly sensitive, private personnel
information.

The form may be copied and a copy given to the complainant for his
or her files. The complainant should agree not to otherwise reproduce or
disclose the form to a co-worker.

Witnesses and Questions

Before you begin the investigation, list the individuals you plan to interview and put them in a tentative order, noting the approximate time each
interview should take. Allot adequate time for important interviews, espe-

cially because new issues often arise early in the investigation. Interviews with complainants and respondents can be lengthy. It is best to allow a half-day for each interview. If you do not need the full half-day, you can use the extra time to write statements and do other preparation work. If you need more time, schedule a second meeting as soon as possible. Witness interviews will go much faster. Interviews with witnesses who have a good deal of direct knowledge could take one to two hours. Interviews with witnesses who have less direct knowledge usually take thirty minutes to an hour. Of course these are just guidelines—every situation differs.

One way to schedule is to keep witnesses on call for a particular day. Schedule the first witness and then contact subsequent witnesses as needed. Schedule witnesses who may discuss the complaint among themselves as closely as possible to avoid them speaking to each other between interviews. It is best to work in as short a time period as possible. A simple investigation could take a day or two whereas a more complicated one might take a week or even longer.

The complainant almost always should be interviewed first. The respondent almost always should be interviewed right after the complainant (allowing for whatever arrangements are necessary to prevent the awkwardness of them seeing each other). If you will interview anyone before the complainant and respondent, have a very good reason to do so. You should have a reason for interviewing everyone on your list. Avoid superfluous interviews—you want to keep the investigation as confidential as possible.

Former employees often are good witnesses because they no longer fear repercussions for being forthright. But you have less control of former employees in terms of assuring privacy, and it may be more difficult to schedule interviews. Think carefully before deciding to interview a former employee. If it is the best way for you to get the information you need and the employee no longer lives in the area, you may conduct some interviews by phone. You also may need to interview witnesses who do not work for your organization, such as clients, customers, or vendors. If you will interview people from outside the organization, think through the approach you will take in contacting these people and soliciting their cooperation. You may need to send a request for the interview to someone who has management authority where the witness is employed. You also should consider how contacting external witnesses may affect the confidentiality of the investigation. In some cases you may decide not to interview certain witnesses if the information they may provide is not significant and if confidentiality or business relations could be seriously compromised.

Prepare a list of questions to ask and a checklist of what you will need to tell each witness about topics such as confidentiality, retaliation, and so forth. You won't follow the list of questions precisely, because during the interview you will need to follow up certain information with other questions. You never know exactly where an interview will lead. Keep a running list of questions for your reference, however, because you likely will add items with each witness you interview. Later on you may need to re-interview earlier witnesses to solicit information on the added items. Your list of questions acts a checklist to help you be sure you cover everything. Creating this list of questions ahead of time also gives you an opportunity to think about difficult issues that may arise.

Coordination and Confidentiality

Investigators often work with a coordinator, who arranges for witness availability and acts as liaison with outside agencies, legal counsel, or law enforcement authorities. The coordinator should be neutral and unbiased, and should convey respect for the process and all the people involved. In some cases, you may want the department manager or another executive who has authority for the workgroup to be coordinator, especially if the employees are unlikely to take direction or feel comfortable with another person. Do not involve an employee's supervisor as the coordinator if there is any possibility that the supervisor participated in or condoned activity that is the subject of the complaint. Also, it is usually best not to place the complainant's or respondent's direct supervisor in a coordinating role. These supervisors may be needed as witnesses and usually won't appear to be fully neutral.

A senior HR representative often is a good person to serve as a coordinator by virtue of his or her experience handling confidential situations. Whomever takes on this role, it is important for that individual to tell the employee only that he or she will be spoken to about a personnel matter, without divulging any other information. It is best to do this in a way that avoids attracting the attention of co-workers. The coordinator should make no comments regarding the subject of the investigation and should not speculate about what the employee will be asked. Making contact orally is usually the best practice because the coordinator's tone of voice can put people at ease and help alleviate concerns. However, Figure 12 illustrates how a sample memo can be used to inform witnesses of an investigation.

Figure 12. Sample Memo Initiating Investigation

Date: _____

To: _____

From: _____

Subject: Investigation Commencing

In the next several days you may be contacted by [investigator's name] to participate in an investigation of a complaint made pursuant to our organization's policy that prohibits harassment. The investigation is an important process for the organization and your cooperation is vital to its success. Our organization expects that you will cooperate fully and give accurate information in response to the investigator's questions. All interviews will be conducted voluntarily and in a way that protects the privacy of everyone involved to the maximum extent consistent with conducting a thorough investigation. Thank you in advance for your cooperation.

Take steps to prevent "informal" side investigations. Some supervisors will want to conduct their own inquiry into what occurred. The interference of an untrained or biased supervisor is a bad idea. When a union steward or business representative is conducting a parallel investigation of a complaint involving a union member, do not allow that investigation to interfere with the one you are conducting. The investigator should contact organizational leaders or legal counsel immediately if he or she finds that side investigations are taking place. Never permit respondents to conduct witness interviews. The employer must maintain the final responsibility to respond to harassment.

Other Participants

A complainant, respondent, or witnesses may want to have a representative or friend present during the interview. As a general rule, investigators should make every effort to conduct the interviews without having others present. But the most important thing is for the investigation to proceed. A determination should be made on a case-by-case basis; if the complainant refuses to be interviewed without having someone present, generally it is best to allow the interview to move forward.

When a party or witness insists on having someone present, the representative, relative, or friend must agree not to interfere (for example, not to try to answer questions for the complainant or challenge the investigator's questions). If the complainant is a minor, it is appropriate to have a parent or guardian present. A recent National Labor Relations Board (NLRB) ruling has extended the right to have another employee present to nonunion employees (but not supervisors) who are, or may be, the subject of disciplinary intervention. Accordingly, requests by a respondent to include another person in the interview should be granted. Because of the potential for intimidation, do not allow a supervisor to be present when an employee is being interviewed.

When you interview witnesses you want to do everything possible to ensure that you get reliable information that is not influenced by someone else's viewpoint. Always interview witnesses separately.

Representatives and Translators

Union Representatives. Employees who are members of a union have a right to representation if there is a possibility that the investigation will lead to disciplinary action against them.

Witnesses who are members of a union also may request representation; these requests should be considered on a case-by-case basis. In general, employees are not entitled to representation unless there is a possibility that they will be disciplined.

You are not required to inform a witness who is a member of a union of his or her right to representation. If the witness requests representation, however, you should evaluate whether allowing union representation will help move the investigation forward or lead to undue interference. Some witnesses will cooperate more fully if they are permitted representation. If you are in doubt as to how to proceed when an employee requests representation, consult your employer's legal counsel or a labor relations specialist.

Lawyers. Rarely, either the complainant or the respondent will request that his or her attorney be present. When this happens it is best to try to work with the lawyer for either party rather than to lose the opportunity to interview an important witness. No court has ruled that a party has a right to an attorney present, but you don't want such a request to become an obstacle that thwarts the investigation. Be sure to let your organization's legal department or outside counsel know if an employee will bring his or her attorney to an investigation interview.

Lawsuits have come about from situations in which a complainant wanted his or her lawyer present for the investigative interview and the employer refused, resulting in the investigation not going forward. Complainants in this situation have filed lawsuits alleging that no action was taken by the employer. Although an employer might respond that it was the complainant who thwarted the investigation in this type of situation, a jury may very well find that the investigation should have gone forward.

If having an attorney present will adversely affect your ability to conduct an investigation, it is best for the employer to find an investigator who will be able to proceed even with the attorney present. This usually means hiring an outside investigator.

Translators. Some investigations will involve participants whose spoken English is limited. In other instances participants may have English as their second language, and sometimes it's difficult to fully understand someone in his or her second language.

Having a competent translator is one solution to these problems. It is best to use a translator from outside the organization who is not acquainted with any of the parties and who has experience as a translator in administrative or judicial proceedings. Inexperienced translators tend to insert their own thoughts and interpretations rather than translating verbatim.

Or, the employer may prefer to have an investigator who can speak the complainant's or respondent's language and conduct the interview in his or her native tongue.

Spouses and Significant Others

Because you want both the complainant and the respondent to be comfortable, you may therefore be inclined to allow either party to bring a companion to the interview if he or she feels a strong need for it. But you should be wary of allowing a spouse or significant other to be present. Because of the extremely close connection, the presence of spouses or significant others is likely to inhibit the parties or influence what they say. Spouses and significant others are more likely than other companions to become emotional during the interview and may have difficulty sticking to the ground rule not to interject or "speak for" the complainant. Questions that could potentially embarrass the parties in front of their spouses or significant others (or even reveal facts that compromise the relationships) may come to light because the issues pertain to the complaint and must be discussed.

Chapter 5 Self-Check

This chapter has provided guidelines to help you plan investigations of workplace harassment. To further your knowledge, complete this exercise: Review the following scenario and jot down questions that you, as the investigator, would use when interviewing the complainant. Ask a colleague to do the same. Compare your list of questions with that of your colleague. Compare your lists with the sample list of suggested questions provided in Appendix A.

Scenario: Harassment on the Basis of Religion

Michael alleges that he has been harassed because he converted to Islam and changed his name to Jamal. He used to get along well with George, the lead worker, until George was planning the schedule and Jamal told him he no longer celebrates Christmas. Jamal says that when he was eating lunch, co-workers made fun of what he was eating and asked him if he was going to start wearing a turban. Jamal says that the pictures he puts up in his area of the tool room are always gone by the time he comes to work the next day.

CHAPTER 6

Documentation

It is the best HR practice to thoroughly document the investigation. You document for the present so that as you proceed with the investigation you can go back and review everything before making a determination. You also document for the future because, should the investigation be called into question, your documentation will show what was done and why you reached your conclusions. Keep your notes, even if you type them up later. The original handwritten notes may be needed in the future. Throwing them away could appear like you are trying to hide something. Remember that everything you write during an investigation will most likely be "discoverable" (open to litigants and their counsel) if a lawsuit is ever filed in relation to your investigation.

When to Start

Begin documentation with the first contact you receive about the investigation. Later it may be important for you to explain the timing and sequence of your initial investigation steps. If an investigation is delayed because of circumstances beyond your control, you will be on better footing if you can show when you started and why. For example, if you delayed the investigation by a week because the complainant said he or she was unavailable, contemporaneous notes of what he or she said (and how you responded) could be helpful in countering an accusation that it was you who caused the delay.

What to Document

There is no such thing as too much documentation. Too little documentation is a common problem. When in doubt, write it down. No one's memory is as good as he or she thinks it is. Information that you think will be indelibly planted in your memory often is forgotten just days later. Also, a detail that you think is too unimportant to write down may turn out to be very important indeed. You will likely hear different versions of the same story. It's easy to become confused about who said what. For all these reasons, it's best not to edit but simply to write down everything. Of course, unless you take shorthand, you can't write down every word. But you can, using abbreviations, write down most of what you are told.

How to Document

Information that is particularly significant should be taken down in the words of the interviewee. Place quotation marks around words that come directly from the interviewee so that you can distinguish his or her words from your paraphrases.

Developing some shorthand and abbreviations will help you take down more information quickly. One good method for tracking a number of different allegations is to assign a number to each allegation and consistently refer to it by number in your notes. By doing this you can be sure that you cover all the allegations and you need not rewrite the allegations each time you refer to them. For example, in your notes, you can write, "Response to allegation 1 - . . ." or, even shorter, "Resp. to # 1 . . . ." Some investigators use the initials of frequently used proper names to speed note taking during interviews. If you use initials make sure to keep a legend of the names and your abbreviation for each. A sample of investigator's notes appears in Figure 13.

Document Objective Facts

Document the actual information you are told in the interviews—not your thoughts and impressions about that information. Your thoughts and impressions may change, but the facts will stay the same. If you have questions about something or want to go back to it, by all means make some sort of notation. But refrain from writing down your subjective impressions. Some investigators place a symbol in the margin of their notes for items they want to go back to later.

One way to think about this is to document the objective facts (including the impressions other people—the parties and witnesses—state to you) but not your own subjective feelings. Remember that if the complaint is not

Figure 13. Sample Notes Page

On this sample page, the investigator's questions and notes appear in regular type. Comments made by the interviewee appear in italic type.

Name of interviewee: _____

Date: _____   Page ____ of ____

Two incidents
Incident #1
"First time he touched my leg when he was reaching beneath the counter"

    Which counter?
      Front cash register
      Only room for one person to stand

    Respondent say anything?
      He mumbled something

    Specifically recall?
      Sounded like "you're hot" or "how hot"

        Did you say anything in response?
          Too shocked
          May have said "that's gross"

    Others in area?
      Customer–handling return
      Seemed to know something had happened

        Customer say anything?
          "Are you all right?"
      Co-worker came 10 to 20 minutes later to relieve for break

        Did you discuss what happened?
          Not right then but later that day after respondent left
          She said "You look upset"
          Told her what happened
            She said she won't go in back room when respondent is there by himself

    Ever discuss touching incident with respondent?
      "No, I feared for my job"

Incident #2
"Second time, I was sitting on the bench next to the candy machine in the break room"

    Always took break at same time
      I have to check with respondent if he is on premises before I take my break
        Told him going on a break
      Usually in the break room by myself

successfully resolved it may end up in litigation. If this happens, your notes will be scrutinized. A stray impression that you document during the investigation could prove embarrassing or difficult to explain later in court.

Get Written Statements

Usually it is best to have each party and witness sign a written statement. Doing this assures that if you have misunderstood what was said in the interview, the party or witness has an opportunity to read and change it. It also prevents parties and witnesses from coming back later and saying you misunderstood or did not get complete information.

The statement need not include everything the witness told you. Rather, it can focus on the relevant facts. Ideally the statement should be in the party's or witness's own words. This does not mean that each party or witness should write his or her statement, but rather that you should write the statements using each person's words and perspective as much as possible. A good witness statement will include the witness's version of the facts in dispute and other facts that you believe are—or will become—relevant. The statement should express what the party or witness was trying to express in the interview.

Example #15

The Paraphrased Statement

Sarah complains about a hostile working environment in the drafting work group. Peter is assigned to investigate. Paul, one of the employees in that unit, tells Peter that there has been occasional swearing but it hasn't been aimed at any one person. He also says he hasn't heard what he would consider "dirty" jokes or jokes about sex. Peter prepares a statement for Paul to sign. It reads, "The work environment in the drafting work group is highly professional. I have never heard anything that could be considered a hostile work environment."

Is this statement well written? How would you write it?

Here, the investigator has glossed over what Paul has said about occasional swearing. The investigator may be concerned that putting down information about the swearing will make it look worse than it should, in light of the fact that Paul has said the swearing is only occasional and isn't aimed at anyone. But leaving out this important fact is evidence of Peter's bias and will make things worse. Peter also has substituted his own words and phrases, such as "highly professional" and "hostile work environment," in the statement. These aren't Paul's words and they have no place in Paul's statement. Essentially, Peter has written his own statement, not Paul's. This is a mistake.

You can use a variety of techniques to take down a statement. If you write neatly and fairly completely, you may be able to have the witness simply review and sign your notes. Some people conduct interviews with a laptop and type the statements in as they go. Other people find that using a computer interferes with their ability to establish rapport with the person they are interviewing.

If you don't think it's realistic to write the statement as you go, you will have to prepare it after the interview. The more time that elapses between the interview and the writing of the statement, the more difficult the task will become. If possible, prepare the statement right away—either while your interviewee waits or while he or she takes a break. The statement can be handwritten or typed, depending on how comfortable you are with each method.

Always allow the people you have interviewed to review what you have written and make any changes they want. Even if an individual wants to change something he or she said, he or she should be permitted to do so, provided the change is obvious on the statement itself. Changes and corrections should be lined through, not obliterated. An interviewee may wish to change something because you truly misunderstood a point or got something wrong (like a spelling correction) or he or she may decide that the interview revealed too much and want to retract or change something that was said. You will have to factor in the fact that a change was made when you evaluate the information provided by the witness. You also can comment on the change in your written report.

If you write statements by hand, some interviewees will want you to type theirs into a computer so they can make more changes. Remember—it is your investigation and you can and should set limits on how far you will go to accommodate a party's or witness's requests. It is often more efficient to handwrite a statement than to type it and allow numerous changes. Some people are perfectionists who will insist on grammatical changes. Let them make the changes if they want to, but don't let it affect how you write the statement. You are getting down what they said, not writing a novel.

Sample statements can be found in Appendices C and E.

Giving Out Copies of Statements

Most experts agree that the complainant and respondent have a right to a copy of their own statements. In some states an employee has a right to have anything he or she has signed placed in his or her personnel file. If that is the case in your state, a signed statement probably will fall into this category. Some investigators make it a practice to offer parties a copy of their statements. Other investigators do not offer a copy but will provide one on request. It is not clear that witnesses have a right to their statements—and most don't request them. If a witness does request a copy of his or her statement, it probably is best to provide it. Any person who takes a copy of his or her statement should agree that while the investigation is pending he or she will not show it to other employees or anyone—other than a representative—who might be involved in the investigation. Most investigators will have the witness affirm this verbally. If you have a particular concern about breaches of confidentiality you could ask for a written agreement not to disclose the statement to anyone.

Once the investigation has been completed, the written statements will either be included as an appendix to the final report or, if referred to in the report but not appended to it, they will be maintained in the investigative file.

Taping Interviews

Taping interviews is rarely a good idea. Tape recording might seem to be a good solution if you are not good at taking notes and prefer not to hold up the investigation by taking time up front to record what you hear in the interviews. A tape will provide an accurate record without you having to take notes. This advantage has to be weighed against the limitations of tape recording equipment and the difficulty of retrieving information from cassette tapes. Technical problems frequently lead to an incomplete record. Investigators who use a tape recorder may relax their note taking and then, when technical problems (e.g., a gap in the tape) develop, they are unable to reconstruct the missing material. Taping also is time-consuming. You have to go back and listen to tapes, as opposed to simply checking notes. Moreover, during interviews it is difficult to do everything "on the record." If you stop the tape during portions of the interview, which necessarily occurs when you take a break or turn over the tape, the investigation is vulnerable to legitimate concerns that some information may not have been documented.

Videotaping is even more intimidating than tape-recording. Videotaping also involves the use of a third party (the videographer) in order to accomplish the videotaping. Lastly, videotaping is very expensive. It is therefore also not recommended.

Certain types of employees have a right to have interviews tape-recorded. For example, sworn law enforcement officers in California have this right pursuant to a state law, "The Peace Officers Bill of Rights." Most employees do not have this right and in some states it is not permissible to tape-record without permission. When no requirement or other compelling reason to tape-record interviews exists it generally is a bad idea.

Figure 14 gives a list of documents that an investigator may assemble in the permanent investigation file. These documents will become part of the permanent record of the investigation (the "permanent investigation

Figure 14. Documentation

Document	Copy to
Intake form (if used)	Permanent investigation file
List of questions	Permanent investigation file
List of people to be interviewed	Permanent investigation file
Investigator's note	Permanent investigation file
Complainant's signed statement	Permanent investigation file; complainant (on request); complainant's personnel file
Respondent's signed statement	Permanent investigation file; respondent (on request)
Witnesses' signed statements	Permanent investigation file; witnesses (on request)
Confidentiality agreement (if signed statements are used)	Permanent investigation file; parties who have signed agreement
Investigative report	Appropriate organizational executive(s) and/or legal counsel; respondents (on request and if required under FCRA; see Chapter 4); permanent investigation file
Follow-up letters	Permanent investigation file; personnel file(s) of recipient(s).

file"). Some items may become part of employee personnel files; others will be retained in a secure area used for archiving investigation files.

Most working documents are intended for use by the investigator alone. Copies of some documents—such as their own statements—may be provided to the complainant, respondent, or witnesses on request. Copies must be provided to external investigators, parties' legal representatives, union representatives, members of law enforcement or the courts as directed by legal counsel or required by law.

A complainant's signed statement will be filed in his or her personnel file because this statement is a full explanation of the complaint. The respondent's signed statement will be filed in the permanent investigation file—as will be the statements of other witnesses. The respondent's personnel file will contain a copy of the follow-up letter to establish a record of communication to the respondent as to the determination reached during the investigation.

Chapter 6 Self-Check

This chapter has provided guidelines to help you thoroughly, fairly, and legally document evidence you may gather as part of an investigation. To further your knowledge, consider the following exercise.

For additional practice with note taking and preparing statements, interview friends or co-workers about something important that happened between them and a friend or neighbor or about something unusual that they witnessed. Ask them to choose a topic with which you would not normally be involved. Take notes and have them review your notes for accuracy. Then draft statements, in their words, about the event. Get their honest feedback as to the accuracy of the statements, both factually and in terms of the flavor of what they were conveying. Did you miss something important? Did you put your own gloss on the topic? Try this exercise with a few different people until you receive consistent feedback that your draft statements accurately reflect what they have said.

The Fact-Finding Process

Prepare for the Interviews

You may find it helpful—or necessary—to go look at the place where the conduct allegedly occurred. You may do this before you begin the interviews and you may want to return for another look after you have gathered enough facts to understand the basic allegations and response. Going to the scene will help you understand who could have seen or heard what happened, what impediments there would be to doing so, and so forth. A visit to the scene also may suggest additional questions.

Example #16

Clues from the Scene of the Complaint

Jeff complains that his supervisor, Myra, constantly calls him her "whipping boy." Myra says she made the comment only once, as a joke, because she had heard Jeff refer to himself as "Myra's whipping boy." When the investigator visits Jeff in his office, she notices that Jeff has an actual whip mounted on the wall behind his desk. Seeing the whip puts Jeff's complaint in another context and leads to questions that would not have occurred to the investigator had she not known it was there. For example, when did Jeff put the whip there—before Myra's alleged comments or after? To what extent has Jeff initiated or participated in this "joke?" Could Jeff's actions have led to Myra thinking that her comments were welcome?

In another case—one with no apparent witnesses—an investigator spent some time in the area where the harassing behavior allegedly took place. He noticed people in the area who might have witnessed the behavior and he was able to find a witness who was able to corroborate the complaint.

In nearly all investigations of workplace harassment you will begin your interviews with the complainant. The only exceptions to this are when there is an anonymous complaint or when a complainant is unavailable and will not be available in a reasonable amount of time. For example, the complainant won't be your first interview when an employee voices a complaint about harassment and then quits, refusing to be interviewed under any circumstances. In this situation you should make every attempt to persuade the complainant to reconsider and allow an interview. If that is not possible, however, an investigation should still take place and you should be sure to document your attempts to obtain an interview with the complainant. There may be other victims. Even if the complainant is the only victim, you don't want wrong behavior to go unpunished. And—although this situation is extremely rare—if the complainant fabricated the allegations, you want to uncover the facts to clear the respondent of any suspicion. The employer has a duty to attend to all complaints of harassment. Fortunately, it is the rare case in which the complainant can't be interviewed. In all other circumstances the interviews will begin with the complainant.

Occasionally the complainant will be out on stress leave during the time the investigation will need to take place. It is likely that the reason for the stress leave will be connected to the alleged harassment, so you will need to proceed cautiously with your interview to avoid any charges that you exacerbated the complainant's stress. Contact the complainant and ask him or her if there are any circumstances (such as meeting offsite, including a representative, relative, or friend at the meeting, or some other circumstance) that will make it possible for you to collect the information you need so that the proper steps can be taken relative to the complaint. If the complainant is still reluctant to meet with you, check with the employer's legal counsel and your workers' compensation carrier (if the stress leave is being taken as an occupational injury leave) to determine the feasibility of contacting the complainant's care provider to request his or her assistance in interviewing the complainant.

Once you have interviewed the complainant, you will proceed with more interviews. Usually you will interview the respondent next, followed by witnesses, to the extent that they are necessary.

Most interviewing techniques apply to all witnesses. Still, you should keep some special considerations in mind when interviewing the complainant and the respondent.

Start with Standard Admonitions

Begin each interview with an introduction that includes certain standard admonitions. The particular admonitions will vary depending on whether you are interviewing the complainant, the respondent, or a witness. Make a checklist of all the standard introductory items that apply to your investigation and check each item off as you start each interview. A standard introduction includes information and admonitions that address

- the purpose of the interview;
- the role of the investigator as a neutral party who will be doing fact-finding;
- the relatively informal nature of the interview, including the fact that the party or witness may take breaks when he or she needs to;
- the employer's expectation that employees will cooperate in investigations and provide accurate information to the best of their ability;
- the fact that the investigator has not reached any conclusion and that the investigator's questions should not be interpreted as implying that he or she believes the allegations;
- an explanation of the employer's expectations about confidentiality, including the investigator's commitment to keep the matter as confidential as possible and the interviewee's commitment, during the course of the investigation, not to discuss the matter with anyone who works for the company other than the investigator;
- an explanation of the employer's duty not to retaliate and the interviewee's duty not to retaliate against anyone in any way for participating in the investigation, along with the interviewee's statement that he or she understands this and will comply; and
- an explanation that that the investigator will take notes and may make them into a statement for the interviewee to sign.

Some (but not all) investigators tell participants that the interview is voluntary (see Figure 15). It is a good idea to have each party and witness—along with anyone representing a party or witness—confirm his or her willingness to abide by the confidentiality requirement. Some investigators get this agreement in writing while others think that doing so is a bit intimidating and conflicts with the investigator's need to establish trust and rapport. Asking participants to verbally agree to keep matters related to the investigation confidential is an acceptable practice. When discussing retaliation, it is imperative that the respondent understand that—regardless of the legitimacy of the complaint—he or she may not take any action against any party, including making comments, starting or spreading rumors, conducting his or her own investigation, or any other action.

Figure 15. Voluntary Participation in Investigations

Employees are expected to cooperate in investigative interviews. An employee who does not cooperate can be subject to disciplinary measures appropriate to insubordination. For this reason, some legal and HR experts do not view investigative interviews as being "voluntary." Other experts argue that such interviews are voluntary because, although there may be job-related consequences, the employees are free to leave at any time. Telling employees that participation in the interview is a voluntary process may put them at ease. In practice, employees rarely refuse to participate in the interviews, whether or not they are told that participation is voluntary.

Sample introductory remarks for interviews with complainants, respondents, and witnesses are provided in Appendix D. After the introductory remarks, the investigator should find out if the party or witness has any questions or concerns—and address those questions or concerns. The investigator also should check to be sure witnesses feel comfortable and, if not, attempt to take whatever steps are necessary to make them reasonably comfortable. Of course most people will not feel fully comfortable with the process. The point is to put the interviewees at ease to the greatest extent possible. If the interview takes place near a lunch period or toward the end of the witness's normal quitting time, prearrange a stopping point and arrange to resume the interview at a later time.

Guidelines for Conducting Interviews

The importance of effective listening throughout your witness interviews cannot be overstated. At times the complainant's most pressing need will be to tell what happened to him or her and how he or she felt about it. Your ability to be an active listener is an important interpersonal communication skill that you will use as you engage with witnesses during the investigation.

Attending to the following information-gathering principles will help make your interviews smoother and more productive. The following tips will apply in most situations.

Maintain Neutrality

It may be hard not to feel sympathy for a complainant who appears to have been mistreated. It may be equally hard not to feel outrage toward a respondent if you believe he or she has done something disrespectful. There is nothing wrong with feeling concern and sympathy for the people you interview. Nor is there anything wrong with feeling angry toward people who have mistreated others. But expressions of concern easily can be misunderstood as compromising your impartiality. Expressions of anger certainly will alienate any witness. Your manner toward the complainant should not be callous; in fact, you should exercise great sensitivity. But be careful not to cross the line and become an advocate or a friend. When interviewing someone who you believe has done something you disapprove of, remember to keep an open mind. You can't stop your feelings, but you can be aware of them and make whatever effort is necessary to hold them in check.

Maintain Emotional Equilibrium

Complainants, respondents, and even witnesses may become upset or angry during an investigative interview. An effective investigator allows people to express their feelings without being distracted from the task of gathering information. You can use techniques like affirming the party's feelings when this occurs. For example, you might say, "I can see that this is very difficult for you" or "I can understand how angry hearing these allegations would make you." Paraphrasing back what a party has said can help the party feel that he or she has been heard and understood. Try very hard not to argue with interviewees or engage these negative emotions. If things start to get out of hand, remember that you can always take a break.

You may be surprised or even angry with some of what you learn during an investigation. You will have to keep those responses to yourself. Do not telegraph your feelings. A hostile party will not be helpful and will not feel fairly treated if your feelings are apparent. *Your job is to be fair to both parties.*

Ask Open-ended Questions

The best way to obtain accurate information is to ask open-ended questions. Journalists refer to these types of questions as the "five W's"—who, what, where, when, and (sometimes) why. Close-ended questions suggest the answer you are seeking and imply what you think the other party is thinking. By asking open-ended questions you will get the interviewee's story in his or her words. Beware the "why" questions, such as "Why didn't you tell someone sooner?" These questions may make someone defensive by implying he or she acted inappropriately. This caution does not mean you should never ask why. Rather, be aware that the word can put someone on the defensive, so it is best not to ask it immediately and to phrase the question carefully. For example, you might say, "I'd like to understand more about what happened. Can you tell me why you responded the way that you did?" Remember, if a party or witness senses that you are disbelieving or unsympathetic, he or she probably will "shut down" and not tell you everything. He or she also will feel your investigation has not been fair and neutral.

Get the Facts

As the investigator, you must insist that witnesses and parties describe events with specificity rather than in summaries or conclusions. It is important to understand the role of interpretation in allegations of sexual harassment. People interpret each other's comments and actions differently depending on many variables, including their relationships with each other, the context, and the perception of intent by one person in relation to another. Making a determination in a harassment complaint often involves the investigator using his or her judgment about the reasonableness of the interpretations made by witnesses. This is why it is important to get the facts of what occurred, not just a witness's conclusion. Witnesses often speak in terms of their conclusions about what occurred rather than stating factually what they observed. A witness may find it hard to tell the difference between "Barbara harassed Jim" and "Barbara was constantly commenting on Jim's appearance by saying 'you have great buns.'" Ask for the details. Apply your skill to ferret out the difference between the conclusions made by various witnesses and the facts.

Ask Background Questions

It is best to start each interview with background questions about witnesses and their relationship to the organization. You will gain some useful information, but, more importantly, you will be able to put the interviewee at ease. During this time you also will have an opportunity to view how witnesses respond to questions that they have no reason to evade. This behavior is what interviewing experts call "baseline behavior," and you will use it as one guideline as you make credibility determinations. More information about baseline behavior and other techniques for weighing information appears in Chapter 8.

Get the Details

Ask for enough detail from the complainant so that you have a full understanding of the allegations and the response. Don't be embarrassed if you must go back over a point and say you don't understand exactly what happened. Doing this will both assist in your understanding and give you the opportunity to see if the interviewee is consistent with his or her account. Walk witnesses through the sequence of events. If appropriate, ask the witness to demonstrate what happened. Repeat back what you heard and ask the witness to either confirm that you got it right or correct any inaccuracies. At the end of the interview, ask the complainant or respondent to list witnesses that he or she thinks you should talk to and *why* he or she thinks you should talk to them. (Witnesses also may be able to suggest additional witnesses.) You may not speak with all these witnesses, and you should tell the party this. But you will want to have a good reason for not talking to a witness if a party expresses strongly you should interview that person.

Obtaining a thorough statement from the complainant is crucial. You need to have a detailed account of what he or she is alleging. Do not assume anything. You want to go into the interview with a clear idea of what you need to get out of it and you want to follow all leads assiduously. Often you will realize later that you do not sufficiently understand a point. It is perfectly acceptable to go back and ask more questions, but to prevent alienating parties and witnesses, you don't want to do that too many times.

It may be important to allow those you interview to discuss previous incidents involving the complainant or respondent even though the incidents may have occurred years before the current complaint. This history may be relevant to the complaint and you should take the time to collect such information. On relevant issues, you will need to get the same level of detail from each witness. One of the challenges of an investigation is staying on track and knowing which issues must be explored in great detail and which are ancillary. Remember, these interviews may be lengthy. Take breaks as needed.

Don't Make Promises You Can't Keep

Often the parties will want you to provide assurances of what action the company will take. If you believe the harassment occurred and was serious, you may be tempted to assure the complainant that the respondent will be fired. If you believe that someone was wrongly accused, you may want to assure him or her that no adverse action will be taken. Be careful not to do either. Until the investigation is complete a determination as to what occurred is premature. Despite your initial feelings you may find that the conduct did *not* occur. If you've made any assurances to either party, you'll be in a very awkward position—and you'll have opened the employer up to liability. It certainly is appropriate to say that the organization takes these complaints seriously and will investigate swiftly and thoroughly. It also is okay to agree to stay in touch with the parties throughout the process. Other than that, avoid promising anything.

Stay on Track

Complainants, respondents, and witnesses may have other issues they want to air. The respondent may have complaints about the complainant or other people at work, may be very focused on finding out who complained, or may insist on knowing what you are going to do about the complaint. Witnesses may want to know the details of the complaint. You can answer some of these questions, but you cannot answer others.

You must provide clear guidance about what you can do and say, and what would be inappropriate. If an interviewee goes off track, you must bring the discussion back to the agenda. All of the complainant's allegations need to be responded to. Some side issues that come up can be tabled for later, while others will be outside the scope of the investigation. If relevant, side issues can be dealt with during the course of the investigation, perhaps in another interview.

You may have to make judgment calls as to which issues to include and which to save for later, so be sure you understand the priority of information you are seeking: allegations, responses to allegations, and corroborating information. You can always go back and widen the scope of an investigation if necessary.

You may find that you need to consult with someone else to determine which issues to include and which to exclude. If an interview is getting too bogged down or an interviewee is taking over the direction of the interview, take a break. Determine where you want to go with the interview, and then set up a new time to resume. When you begin again, do so with a clear message as to the scope of the interview. When a witness persists in discussing topics that are not relevant to the scope of your investigation, it can be helpful to make a list of those areas with the witness.

Making such a list can serve to reassure the interviewee that you, the investigator, have "heard" him or her even though you are not committing to follow through with matters outside the scope of the investigation. Once a witness feels that he or she has been heard in this manner, the witness often will be more willing to return to and stick with the information-gathering you need to perform for the investigation. Later, perhaps with the cooperation of the witness, you can decide whether to forward the list of other matters to an appropriate authority in HR or management.

Interview the Complainant

Complainants present special challenges for the investigative interviewer. These challenges arise because of factors inherent in the situation of the person who brings a complaint. Dealing successfully with these challenges can make a big difference in the quality of your investigation.

Handling Special Requests for Confidentiality

At times an employee will tell a supervisor or human resource manager about workplace harassment but ask that the matter be kept confidential. Even later, during the investigation interview, a complainant may not want the investigator to divulge certain details of the complaint. You cannot agree to do this. Once the employer has been notified of allegations of harassment, action must be taken—and therefore the matter cannot be kept absolutely confidential (but see the discussion of confidential intake and informal resolution systems in Chapter 2). If a complainant asks you to keep details of the allegations confidential, keep in mind the following points.

- Most people do not speak to someone about harassment unless they want something to be done. It is likely that the complainant does want you to take action and realizes that that will mean telling someone else about the problem.

- The statement "don't tell anyone" is a complainant's way of raising concerns about privacy and how the matter will be handled. If you address those concerns, the complainant's hesitations may disappear. Ask questions like, "What would you need to feel comfortable going forward with this complaint?" "What do you fear will happen if you make a complaint?" or "What can the employer do to make you more comfortable going through the complaint process?"

- Most complainants will understand the principle of fairness that requires you to get the "other side of the story." They realize that you will interview the respondent. Sometimes a complainant will feel more comfortable if he or she is assured of being notified when the respondent is going to find out about the complaint. The complainant may want to take a day off that day. An offer of being placed on administrative leave can alleviate some concerns.

- Explaining that harassment tends to become progressively more severe if it is not addressed may help you persuade a complainant to move forward. You may also point out that other victims may be harmed if he or she does not come forward. You can explain that you will attempt to collect enough information from several witnesses so that you do not need to disclose the identity of individuals who gave information.

- Continue attempting to persuade the complainant to participate until he or she feels comfortable with doing so. Ultimately, if the individual does not want to cooperate but the allegations are anything but trivial, you will still need to conduct an investigation.

Handling Questions about Employer Action

Remember, while you do want to persuade the complainant to come forward, you can't promise what the result of the investigation will be or what actions the employer will take. Some investigators ask the complainant what he or she would like to see happen as a result of the investigation. Doing this reassures the complainant that you are considering his or her feelings and the complainant's answer may help you determine the level of seriousness the complainant ascribes to the allegations. If you ask this question, however, be careful to convey that it is not up to the complainant or to you to decide disciplinary action. Some employers make the mistake of leaving it up to the complainant to determine what action to take so that if the complainant says an apology is sufficient or that he or she wants no action taken, the employer complies. Yet if the investigation yields a finding that serious harassment occurred, these responses would be inadequate.

The fact that a complainant suggests a minor form of discipline may lull an employer into thinking this would be adequate. But if the harassment continues—or even if the complainant later realizes he or she is uncomfortable working around the respondent—the complainant may later say he or she felt pressured into agreeing to a solution that would not adversely impact the perpetrator. Also, if the perpetrator of the harassment goes on to harass someone else, that employee could complain that the perpetrator should have been terminated (or at least disciplined more severely) when the employer first learned of the earlier harassment. The final decision about disciplinary action always is best left to the employer. Disciplinary action is covered more fully in Chapter 10.

Interview the Respondent

Your approach to interviewing the respondent should be much like your approach to interviewing the complainant. You may find it difficult to remain impartial. After hearing the complainant's story, most people form a mental picture of the respondent and it is hard not to make assumptions about what occurred. Remember that everyone you interview should be approached respectfully and with an open mind.

Defensiveness is a natural posture of people accused of wrongdoing regardless of whether they are guilty of the allegations. It is safe to assume that the respondent will respond defensively. If you can help the respondent get over feeling defensive, the interview will proceed more easily. Pointing out that you have not yet made a determination and will need the respondent's cooperation to understand the facts often is enough to do this.

A respondent sometimes will react to learning of the complaint with utter surprise. Most respondents will indicate that they had no intent to offend anyone. The respondent may genuinely not have understood that certain behavior was offensive and therefore may want to speak to the complainant right away in an effort to resolve the situation. Such a reaction, while understandable in some circumstances, must be handled firmly with an instruction not to do so. At a later date this type of discussion or apology may be appropriate.

Where to Start

When you go over the standard admonitions with the respondent and you discuss the purpose of the investigation, you will not want to reveal the precise allegations. You will say something general to the effect that there has been a complaint implicating the respondent in possible workplace harassment and you will be asking questions and gathering facts. The respondent will want to know all the details—but revealing too much at this early point in the interview can derail your investigation. You can assure the respondent that you will inform him or her of all the allegations by the end of the interview, but be firm in staying on track.

The complainant's allegations will form the basis for your interview of the respondent. You do have an obligation to tell the respondent what has been alleged and to give the respondent an opportunity to respond to each allegation. But it is a good practice to save the more difficult questions for the end of the interview. The less confrontational you are at the start of the interview, the more information you will gain.

Make sure you cover all the allegations by the end of the interview. Inform the respondent what the specific allegations are and get his or her response to each allegation. While you are not obligated to tell the respondent who complained (and in fact should keep that information confidential if possible), the respondent usually will be able to figure it out from your questions. Sometimes the person who makes the complaint is different from the person being harassed. The respondent will almost always need to know who is involved in the allegations but should be reminded that that is not necessarily the person who complained.

Begin with neutral questions about the respondent's job, history with the company, relationships with co-workers, and so forth. Proceed to questions that ask about the work environment and the relationships between employees. In hostile environment sexual harassment cases you may consider asking general questions about the environment, such as how the respondent would describe the civility in this environment compared to others, what level of profanity and sexual references are acceptable, and what are his or her use of profanity and sexual references in general.

A critical element of unlawful harassment is that the behavior was unwelcome. Accordingly, you need to collect sufficient information about the nature of the relationship between the complainant and the respondent to ascertain whether the behavior was or was not welcome. You need to understand, to the best of your ability, what the respondent understood about his or her relationship with the complainant that may have justified the behavior you are investigating. This includes asking about whether they had a relationship outside of work and what that relationship consisted of. Some sexual harassment complaints emanate from employees who formerly dated. The fact that they dated does not mean there cannot be harassment, but it is relevant to understanding the allegations.

Example #17

When Is a "Friend" Not a Friend?

Nabil's work productivity has declined. When questioned about this he brings up the fact that his co-worker, Ted, calls him derisive names such as "camel jockey" and, instead of calling Nabil by name, refers to him as "Mohammed." Nabil has begun avoiding Ted, which makes it difficult for Nabil to perform effectively at work.

When Ted is interviewed he says he thought Nabil and he were friends. According to Ted, they have joked together about Nabil's national origin. Ted says he had no idea Nabil found the comments offensive. When the investigator goes back and questions Nabil, Nabil admits that he never told Ted to stop the comments and perhaps he acted like they were okay, but only because he didn't want to make waves.

Here, Ted's ignorance and insensitivity led to a hostile work environment for Nabil. His notion of "friendship" was quite different from Nabil's. This difference in perspective led to a situation that had a negative impact on Nabil's work. Clear guidance about what types of comments are acceptable at work and "sensitivity" training are ways to help alleviate this situation.

Maintain Confidentiality

The respondent does not have a right to know who complained. However, it is natural for him or her to want to know this information. You may need to explain your obligation not to reveal more information than is necessary to do a thorough investigation. In most cases the respondent will know or correctly assume who has complained. The respondent may still ask questions about what witnesses have said and what information you, the investigator, have learned. Although you cannot reveal confidential information, you can acknowledge how difficult it is to be in the respondent's position. As with the complainant, a little understanding goes a long way to reassure the respondent that you are conducting a fair and neutral investigation.

Interview Witnesses

Once you have completed thorough interviews of both parties, you usually will interview witnesses. It is possible, though rare, to come to a determination after interviewing only the complainant and respondent. If the respondent admits the behavior and there is no evidence of actions affecting other victims, further interviews probably will not be necessary. Occasionally, there simply are no witnesses who can add anything to an investigation, even if conduct is denied. In these rare cases you will need to make a determination without further interviews. In most cases, even if there is no direct witness to the alleged behavior, other types of witnesses will be able to shed some light on the allegations and should be spoken to.

Where to Start

When questioning a witness you usually will start with the preliminary admonitions. When you explain the investigator's role, be sure not to reveal any more detail than is necessary.

At times when questioning a witness you will *not* go through the formal admonitions. For example, in investigating a complaint of environmental harassment, you may want to question employees who spend a lot of time around the respondent to find out if he or she generally behaves in the manner alleged. If that is the case, you may not need to reveal that a specific complaint has been filed. Rather, you might approach the topic as a general issue that the organization wants more information about. You can focus on an entire workgroup rather than a specific individual. With this line of questioning, the typical admonitions will not always be necessary.

Some witnesses will have a negative attitude about the investigation and may appear to refuse their cooperation. Usually it is best to take the time to determine the basis for their concerns and, using the techniques described above, to attempt to persuade them to cooperate. The self-check exercise at the end of this chapter will help you prepare for several specific witness-directed challenges to your investigation.

Determine Whom to Interview

As is elaborated in Chapter 8, there are different types of witnesses. A "direct witness" is someone who allegedly saw the event described. Direct witnesses generally are the most important and should be interviewed first. "Contemporaneous witnesses" are individuals who did not see the event but who were spoken to about the event shortly after it occurred (contemporaneously with the occurrence of the event). For example a contemporary witness could be a friend or co-worker in whom the complainant confided or someone who saw the complainant upset. Contemporaneous witnesses can be crucial in establishing credibility. There also may be witnesses who can attest to similar behavior on the part of one or the other party. These witnesses generally are not the first choice, but it may be necessary to interview them when other evidence is unavailable.

"Character witnesses" are people who can attest to the general character of an individual, such as their reputation for truthfulness. It is rarely useful to interview character witnesses in a harassment investigation unless the witnesses can shed light on the specific events. Witnesses whom you interview for other purposes may also want to offer "character" information about the complainant or respondent. It is not usually a good idea to solicit this information. You are not conducting the investigation to determine who the better person is, and becoming too involved in character evidence can lead to bias and to a breakdown in confidentiality.

Example #18

Choosing among Potential Witnesses

Monique complains that Carol has been sexually harassing her by asking her out on dates and touching her. You are assigned to investigate. Monique has five witnesses she would like you to interview:

■ Larry, who Monique says saw some of the touching;

■ Jennifer, who Monique says Carol has also asked out;

■ Gertrude and Alice, who Monique says can tell you that Carol is a lesbian; and

■ Monique's friend Barbara, whom she told about the harassment.

You interview Carol first. She states that she is not a lesbian—and besides, her sexual orientation is none of your business. Carol also states that she has not asked Monique or Jennifer out and she may have innocently touched Monique but not because she's interested in her—she isn't! She also tells you Monique is a known slut and has dated Isaac and Mo. She wants you to talk to four witnesses: Isaac and Mo and Jackson and Eloise, who will tell you what a good employee Carol is and to confirm that she is always professional.

Whom do you interview next? Larry. Why? Larry has been named as a direct witness—someone who saw the touching. If further interviewing is necessary, you will then talk to Jennifer because Monique says Carol asked her out. This is an allegation of similar behavior and thus might show a pattern. You also need to determine if Jennifer has experienced any unwanted behavior. You may also want to talk to Barbara because she is a contemporaneous witness.

There is no need to talk to Gertrude or Alice. Whether Carol is a lesbian, straight, or bisexual is irrelevant. The issue is whether there was unwanted touching or unwanted requests for dates. Similarly, there is no need to talk to Isaac and Mo. Whether Monique dates either of them is irrelevant. How about Jackson and Eloise? They don't have information relevant to the specific allegations, but they can provide general character evidence. You may decide to interview Jackson or Eloise just so Carol feels that you have been fair. If you don't interview one of them, you won't have interviewed anyone Carol suggested. Of course if you're going to find in Carol's favor, you don't need to worry about her feeling you've been fair so in that situation you will have no need to interview Jackson or Eloise.

For each case you investigate you will create lists of possible witnesses to interview based on whom the complainant wants you to talk to, whom the respondent wants you to talk to, and your own conclusions as to who might have relevant information. You do not have to interview a witness just because the complainant or respondent wants you to. But you will need to talk to all witnesses who might have information that could help you make a determination as to what occurred and who are necessary for a fair investigation. You do not want to talk to more people than necessary. How can you decide? Start with the most obvious and necessary witnesses. Usually these are witnesses who may have actually seen some of the behavior alleged. See where things go from there. Have a good reason for interviewing everyone you speak to—and have a good reason for not interviewing any witness you were asked to interview but decided not to.

It can be especially difficult to construct a list of interviewees in complaints involving allegations of a hostile environment on the basis of ethnicity or race. Some investigators may want to interview everyone in the workplace or everyone from the nondominant minority groups.

A good way to proceed is to sample the impressions held by people from the various ethnic and racial groups. For example, an African American who complains about racial harassment tells the investigator that all African American employees have experienced racism and there have been open discussions among the African American employees of harassment based on race. The investigator will be justified in interviewing more African American employees than he or she would interview had no information surfaced about the open discussions. If interviewing a few African American employees provides corroboration of this type of widespread harassment, the investigator will continue to expand his or her witness list. On the other hand, if several of the African American witnesses do not corroborate the harassment, the investigator should not continue to expand the list. Instead, he or she should go back to the complainant and give him or her an opportunity to provide specific names of employees who can corroborate the harassment. Those individuals should then be interviewed.

Maintain Neutrality with Witnesses

You also will need to be and appear neutral in interviews with witnesses. Witnesses will be sensitive to how you ask questions. If you exhibit a bias or point of view, they will pick up on it. Many witnesses would prefer not to be involved in an investigation. Treating them with courtesy and showing that you are fair and neutral will make them feel better about the process. This helps the current investigation and makes employees feel they will be treated fairly should they have a complaint in the future.

Maintain Confidentiality

Witnesses will be curious about what is going on. There is nothing wrong with such curiosity, but you must not provide information. Sometimes it is difficult to get information if you don't reveal something about the investigation. This may simply be a logistical problem. For example, in order to orient the witness to what you need to know, you may need to name certain people. You can try to ask general questions and to ask questions about entire workgroups or about numerous people, only some of whom are involved in the complaint. When this approach is feasible, it can effectively preserve confidentiality. If it is not feasible, you may have to reveal some information. Each case will differ. Plan ways that you can get information without having to reveal who has complained or who the complaint is against.

Example #19

Naming Names

Fred complains about retaliation for bringing a harassment complaint based on his age. He says that Antoinette heard his supervisor, Roger, say he was going to "get" him, and that this occurred the day after Fred brought his complaint. When the investigator questions Antoinette by asking general questions, Antoinette has no idea what the investigator was getting at. Has she heard any threats? No. Anything inappropriate? No. Has anyone said they were going to "get" someone else? No. Ultimately the investigator has to ask specifically whether Antoinette heard Roger say he was going to "get" Fred. There is no other way to confirm whether she had heard this.

Even though you have instructed witnesses not to discuss the contents of interviews with each other, sometimes you will discern that witnesses have been talking about the investigation with each other. You will need to think about what effect these discussions may have on the corroboration you are seeking from witnesses. You also may have to consider sanctions for employees who breach the confidentiality of your investigation. If the breach is serious enough, you may believe that disciplinary action is necessary. If that is the case it is a good idea to consult with the employer's legal counsel before determining what action to take. *Depending on the seriousness of the breach of confidentiality, it also may suffice to remind the witnesses of the confidentiality agreement and let them know you are aware they have violated it, giving them a warning that disciplinary actions will be taken if they continue to talk about confidential items.*

A witness who is a supervisor or manager should be told that he or she might learn information in the course of the investigation that he or she wants to act on for the good of the department. He or she should be admonished *not* to take any action until the investigation is concluded and he or she has consulted with the investigator and/or human resources.

Determine the Sufficiency of Evidence

Once you have interviewed all the witnesses on your list, you will need to assess what you have learned and what you don't yet know. Some investigators write out a page for each allegation and list what evidence supports each allegation and what evidence weighs against it. However you organize the information, you need to decide if you have sufficient information to make a determination and—if not—whether more relevant information is potentially available. Perhaps there are witnesses you have not yet interviewed, or you may realize there were questions you didn't think to ask a certain witness. You will need to determine how important the missing information is. Will it make a difference in your findings? Why or why not?

Any missing information that might influence your findings must be obtained. You may re-interview witnesses by telephone. If you are unsure of what a witness was saying during the initial interview, go back and clarify. In the end you will need to make conclusions as to what occurred. Make sure you are comfortable with the amount of information you have to support those conclusions. It is better to be safe than sorry.

Sample interviews with a complainant, respondent, and witness appear in Appendix E. These interviews illustrate useful questioning techniques but are not intended to be complete investigative interviews. The sample interviews are followed by sample notes and sample statements.

Chapter 7 Self-Check

This chapter has provided guidelines for interviewing to gather facts relating to an allegation of workplace harassment. Consider the following "tough questions" that may come up during interviews with complainants, respondents, or witnesses. How would you respond? Check your answers against the suggestions provided in Appendix A.

1. Complainant: "Everyone knows that nothing is going to change around here, so why bother with asking me all these questions?"
2. Complainant: "I don't know why I should have to talk to you. I've told managers about this problem already and all that happened is that I was called a chronic complainer and a bitch."
3. Respondent: "I want to know right now everything that has been said about me, who said it, and all the details of what I supposedly did that was so wrong. My attorney told me not to answer questions until I have this information."
4. Respondent: "(Complainant) has been a troublemaker for years. I'm the first manager that has stood up to it and challenged him (or her).

Now you are accusing me of harassment because I did my job."

5. Witness: "HR is anything but a neutral party around here. Before I say anything, I want to know who you are going to discuss my interview with."

6. Witness: "Two years ago we had an investigation and three of the people who participated got laid off and one person was transferred against his will. What assurances can you give me that I won't be punished in a similar way for answering your questions?"

Weighing the Evidence and Making a Decision

You've gathered all the relevant evidence, spoken to witnesses, and taken statements. Your work is done. Or is it? Now comes the hard part—coming to a determination. Many harassment claims involve the classic "he said, she said" presentation of opposing viewpoints. Even when some facts are admitted, others are disputed; and often there are questions about the meaning of the admitted conduct. After all your questions have been asked and answered, you are put in the challenging position of having to make a determination of what happened and to evaluate the significance of what occurred. Many investigators throw up their hands at this point, and say, "Who can tell?" They decide there isn't sufficient "proof" and therefore that no determination can be made. Thus no action is taken.

What is sufficient proof? It would be nice to have a videotape of what occurred. That isn't likely to happen. Short of that nonexistent video, how much proof do you need? To answer this question we must first look at what *level* of proof is needed in this situation.

Legal Standards

When cases go to court, the party bringing the action (the plaintiff in a civil suit, the state in a criminal action) has the "burden of proof." The level of proof required differs depending on the type of case. Harassment cases almost always are civil actions that are filed under state or federal law by a regulatory agency or a plaintiff against an employer and, at times, an individual. In rare cases (for example when a serious assault is involved) workplace harassment may result in the state bringing criminal charges against the perpetrator.

Proof Beyond a Reasonable Doubt

Beyond a reasonable doubt is the highest level of proof. This is the level of proof necessary in a criminal action. The rationale is that, if the defendant is found guilty in a criminal case, he or she can be placed in jail and his or her freedom can be taken away. In the United States, the highest degree of proof possible is necessary for freedom to be removed. Any reasonable doubt results in a verdict of not guilty.

People often try to apply the phrase "innocent until proven guilty" to a respondent in a harassment investigation. This phrase comes from criminal law in cases where the proof must be beyond a reasonable doubt. Although a widely accepted cultural value, the legal concept of "innocent until proven guilty" doesn't apply in investigations of harassment complaints. The investigator is not trying to establish guilt or innocence, only to determine whether the actions occurred. This is not to say that an employee accused of harassment should be considered "guilty" during the investigation.

Preponderance of the Evidence

In most civil cases, the plaintiff must prove his or her case by a "preponderance of the evidence." This phrase means that in weighing the evidence, it is more likely than not that the alleged action occurred. Some people describe this using an image of the scales of justice. If the scales dip ever so slightly in favor of the plaintiff, he or she will prevail. The judge or jury need not be persuaded beyond a reasonable doubt. A preponderance of the evidence is the level of proof that would be needed in a lawsuit for unlawful harassment under state or federal law. Because a judge or jury would decide a civil lawsuit based on the preponderance of the evidence this should be the standard applied to internal investigations of allegations of workplace harassment.

Some investigators believe that taking away someone's job is equivalent to the death penalty in an employment setting. These investigators may not be comfortable making a finding that allegations of harassment occurred unless they are persuaded beyond a reasonable doubt. An investigator may find it particularly difficult to make a finding that conduct occurred if the respondent repeatedly and adamantly denies the behavior and if the investigator believes that a finding that the conduct occurred will lead to a termination.

An investigator's reticence to make a finding for these reasons often results in no determination being made. Yet in many of these complaints, there would have been sufficient proof that the allegations occurred using the preponderance of the evidence standard. Investigators who insist on finding proof beyond a reasonable doubt put the complainant in a position of having to "prove" to the employer that the harassment occurred based on a more difficult standard than a court would require.

Such an expectation has obvious implications for the employer's liability. If a jury finds, based on a preponderance of the evidence, that the complainant was harassed and that the employer (based on the same set of facts) failed to make a finding, the jury likely will question the employer's good faith and may award significant damages to the complainant.

Example #20

Level of Proof

In one case reported in an HR publication, a female employee informed her employer that a co-worker had attempted to rape her while she was working at the employer's facility after hours. The employee who was accused denied any involvement. The employer did an investigation, discovered there were no witnesses, and decided there was insufficient proof to make a determination. Criminal charges were brought and ultimately a jury found the male employee guilty of attempted rape.

In this investigation the employer was, in all probability, expecting a higher level of proof than was realistic. Because there were no witnesses to the act, the investigator was forced to decide the case based on the credibility of the parties.

If the investigator truly felt both parties were equally credible, the employer should have considered involving the police given the gravity of the charges. The police have the ability to gather evidence (fingerprints and other forensic evidence) that the employer will not have access to. The police also can administer lie detector tests, which the employer cannot do.

In a similar case, the police were brought in and the perpetrator confessed to a sexual assault he had previously denied. This admission occurred after the perpetrator failed a lie detector test and then was questioned by an experienced police investigator.

Many employers falsely believe that if there are no independent witnesses, there can be no finding of harassment. This is not so. The investigator must uncover as much evidence as possible. If the only available evidence is the statement of the accuser and the accused, a determination must be made based on credibility. (Making credibility determinations is discussed further throughout this chapter.)

Sometimes an investigator balks at making a finding that conduct occurred because the investigator has concerns about the effects this conclusion will have on the respondent's career. No one wants to be responsible for destroying someone's career and livelihood, especially when allegations have not been proved "beyond a reasonable doubt." *You should focus on determining whether there is sufficient evidence that the allegations occurred.* Do not concern yourself with what the eventual outcome will be as a result of your findings. Concerns about the impact of investigation findings are properly left to someone other than the investigator, either someone from HR or an organizational leader; otherwise the neutrality of the investigation may be compromised (see Chapter 10). This does not mean that the level of proof developed during the investigation will not be taken into consideration in determining what action to take. But the fact that an investigation has not uncovered proof beyond a reasonable doubt should not deter you from making a finding. The next question is how you will make those findings.

Determining Credibility

In some cases a respondent will admit to the allegations or you will be able to determine that a misunderstanding occurred based on different descriptions of similar facts. Your task becomes more difficult when you cannot reconcile the allegations with the response and the only possible conclusion is that someone is lying. Credibility determinations may be the only basis you have to work with when the respondent denies all the allegations and there are no direct witnesses.

Most cases will involve credibility determinations to some extent. Evidence from some witnesses often directly conflicts with evidence from other witnesses. The investigator must determine who is telling the truth and who is not. Determining the truth from two or more conflicting stories can be a very difficult task. You may have a "gut instinct" and your gut instinct may be correct. But you must support that gut instinct with objective facts. If the facts do not support your feelings, perhaps your instinct was wrong!

Many people believe that they can accurately read body language and tell if someone is lying. In fact, it is very difficult to make credibility determinations based on demeanor alone. A truthful witness may be nervous about being interviewed. An experienced liar can be very good at remaining poised and making eye contact while weaving a tale. In some cultures direct eye contact is considered a sign of honesty; in other cultures direct eye contact is considered rude.

Some people think that if a story has any discrepancies, these discrepancies are indicative of lying. Discrepancies may not be the result of lies, but rather reflect normal lapses in memory. Certainly, you will use judgments about demeanor and observations about discrepancies in testimony to assist you in determining credibility. But you must be aware of the pitfalls of putting too much stock in the person's demeanor alone. With discrepancies, you should consider the significance of—and possible other reasons for—the discrepancies.

Brian Fitch is an experienced police investigator with the Los Angeles County Sheriff's Department. At a training session for lawyers sponsored by the Employment Law Section of the State Bar of California, Fitch explained his investigative technique and how he determines when someone is lying. Some police interrogators use an adversarial style that would be inappropriate for you to use as an internal investigator of employee harassment complaints. Fitch says that he trains investigators in more effective techniques. Fitch focuses on two important things for a successful investigative interview: proper preparation and rapport. At the training session Fitch stated

> First, take time to determine the individual's "baseline" behavior. This is his behavior when he is openly and honestly answering non-threatening questions. Look to things like body posture, use of gestures, eye contact, and the rate, pitch, and tone of his voice. After establishing the person's baseline behavior, the investigator can look for deviations from that baseline when the person answers questions concerning the relevant issue.
>
> Next, in questioning the witness about the relevant issues, look for changes in their baseline behavior, "verbal evasion" and "decep-

tive verbal responses." Human beings' natural tendency is to seek escape from those things that cause discomfort. This can be accomplished by physical distance (flight) or psychological distance (telling a lie, moving away from the interviewer).

Lastly, the fact that you have detected that someone is not telling the truth does not mean they are guilty of what they are being accused of. You may be questioning a man accused of assaulting an employee on a specific date. When asking him where he was, he is evasive. The suspect, in fact, is not being truthful about his whereabouts. However the reason is not because he assaulted the employee but because he was somewhere else—cheating on his wife.

When you question witnesses and try to ascertain their credibility, you can use Fitch's approach, looking for clues in behavior such as

- verbal evasion,
- deceptive verbal responses,
- indirect admissions, and
- body language.

Verbal Evasion

Verbal evasion occurs when the interviewee will not directly answer the question. Many people do not lie outright. Rather, they lie by omission or by not directly answering the question posed. An evasive response may rely on a linguistic loophole (think about former president Bill Clinton's definition of "sexual relations"). One reason you should ask specific questions is that they make verbal evasion more difficult. If an interviewee gives an evasive answer, repeat the question. If after a few repetitions of a direct question the interviewee still will not provide a direct, nonevasive answer, it is likely the person is not being truthful.

Another technique is to notice differences in the way a person answers critical questions versus questions that are not as central to a dispute. For example, an individual may answer a series of questions about his or her involvement in a workplace incident directly by saying "no," yet answer other questions about disputed facts by saying, "I don't recall"—a more indirect, possibly evasive, response. This shift in the style of the answer may be an important item for you to evaluate in some situations. By repeating or rephrasing the question, you give the interviewee an opportunity to expand or explain an answer. If the interviewee continues to be evasive, it is strong evidence that he or she is not providing complete information.

Some witnesses believe, or have been coached to believe, that it is best to feign ignorance of any significant fact. But once you develop rapport with a witness, it is usually difficult for that person to continue providing these types of nonresponsive answers.

Deceptive Verbal Responses

Some answers that appear to be denials actually are couched in ambiguous or qualifying language. Look for phrases such as "not really," "I guess," "I think," "as far as I know." Alternatively, the interviewee may not answer the question at all, saying something instead like "I wasn't even there," "Why would I do something like that?" or "It couldn't have been me." When confronted with such a nonresponse, you should ask the question again, possibly in another way, and give the interviewee an opportunity to answer you directly. Interviewees often evade direct questions by providing nonanswers. Here are some examples.

- Investigator: "Have you told any employee that they should 'shut up and do their work' or you would get someone else who would?"
- Interviewee: "That's not the way I usually handle things when I talk to my subordinates."
- Investigator: "Has there ever been a situation when you have said something like what is alleged?"
- Interviewee: "Not that I am aware of, not generally, no."

Example #21

Evasive Answers

A supervisor has been accused of asking a subordinate out on a date. When the investigative team asks him if he did that he puts up his ring finger and says, "I'm married." When asked again he responds, "I'm a Christian." When asked a third time he replies, "I wouldn't do that." After all the interviews have been concluded, the investigative team ultimately determines that he did ask the subordinate out.

Indirect Admissions

Occasionally respondents will provide an indirect admission by pointing the finger at someone else who, in the respondent's opinion, has done something equally bad or worse than what he or she is alleged to have done. For example, a respondent might say, "Look, you wouldn't believe the stuff other guys say around here." In this case you need to refocus the respondent to answering questions about his or her own behavior. Before doing so, however, you may follow the thread a bit first. There are two reasons to do this: You may learn something about the work environment, and the respondent may feel more comfortable admitting to engaging in behavior when putting it in the context of "what others do."

Body Language

Some nonverbal cues, such as changes in an individual's posture, shifting in his or her seat, stiffening, or looking away when he or she is questioned about something he or she is not being truthful about, can help you in determining credibility. It is important to observe the person's posture (to get a baseline) before you ask questions that may elicit an untruthful response. A person's posture often will shift from an open to a closed position when he or she is discussing sensitive issues. Attending to postural clues can help an investigator evaluate the emotional content of an employee's responses to questions and whether the employee finds particular topics more or less stressful. Figure 16 presents some characteristics typically associated with open and closed posture.

Figure 16. Characteristics of Open and Closed Posture

Open Posture	Closed Posture
Arms uncrossed or loosely crossed	Arms crossed
Good overall eye contact	Poor overall eye contact
Positive facial expressions	Negative facial expressions
Frontal alignment	Body or head angled away
Forward lean	Bored or disinterested
Palms up	Hands clenched into fists
Smooth, fluid changes in position	Creating distance
Proper use of illustrators or gestures	Lack of illustrators or gestures

It also is important to understand that the significance of posture may differ based on the culture of the individual. For example, individuals from some backgrounds may express anger more readily than individuals from other backgrounds. That anger can take a physical form, such as a raised voice, glaring, or table pounding. These physical signals can be misread as presenting a physical threat or exhibiting defensiveness on a topic, when the individual really is just "letting off steam." Investigators can misread responses if an interviewee's demeanor is far different from what their own would be under the circumstances. An investigator from a culture that values deference to people in authority might react strongly to a party whose culture does not promote deferential behavior. The party's physical attitude could be misinterpreted as representing defiance, anger, or defensiveness toward the investigative process—which some investigators might interpret as a lack of credibility. *Be sensitive to cultural and diversity issues that may affect interpersonal communication during interviews.*

Making a Determination

Five common factors that investigators look at when making determinations as to whether a contested fact happened are

- corroboration,
- contradictions,
- whether the facts are inherently improbable,
- whether the witness has a motive to lie, and
- declarations against interest.

Corroboration

If a witness who has little or no motive to lie corroborates an allegation, it is strong proof that the alleged event occurred. There are two types of corroboration—direct corroboration and indirect (or contemporaneous) corroboration.

Direct corroboration can be obtained when a witness actually saw an event. The witness may not have seen the entire incident or noticed other details important to the investigation. He or she may be able to corroborate only that someone *was* present at a certain place and time when that person said he or she was not present. If the witness was unaware that he or she was witnessing something important, it is likely that his or her focus was elsewhere. Hence the witness may have noticed some but not all of the details of the alleged incident. This does not mean the event did not happen the way the witness has described it. People tend to think that if a neutral witness was present at an event, the witness's rendition of the facts should be more accurate than either party's rendition. Certainly witnesses have fewer motives to fabricate or exaggerate, but that does not necessarily mean they clearly witnessed all the significant events. A neutral witness often will be less sensitive to the interaction between other people and, therefore, will fail to notice details that were significant to the people involved in the incident. When you conduct an investigation, thoroughly question witnesses so that you can ascertain how much they were able to observe, what else they were doing at the time, and so forth.

Indirect (or contemporaneous) witnesses are people who were not present at the event but in whom a party confided about what occurred soon after the event, or who saw a party in a given emotional state soon after the event. Sometimes investigators make the mistake of asking only whether an event was directly witnessed. While direct witnesses can provide the strongest corroborating evidence, indirect witnesses also can provide valuable information and their evidence should be given considerable weight as the investigator makes a determination.

Example #22

The Value of Contemporaneous Witnesses

When Anita Hill testified before the Senate Judiciary Committee about Clarence Thomas, she provided names of two or three individuals with whom she spoke about Thomas's harassment at the time the alleged incidents occurred, many years before her testimony before the committee. These individuals were contemporaneous witnesses. Many legal scholars believe that the witnesses who received her contemporaneous reports provided a significant boost to Hill's credibility because she would have had no motive to fabricate the events at the time that she told her friends about them.

Contradictions

Internal contradictions can provide strong evidence that someone is lying. A story may seem plausible when first presented, but on more questioning contradictions may become evident. Uncovering contradictions is one reason for thoroughly questioning—and re-questioning—certain parties and witnesses. To recognize contradictions in an interviewee's responses you will need to listen carefully and make sure you understand exactly what is being said. Be sure your questions are consistent and clear to the interviewee. If questions are ambiguous, inconsistent, or unclear to the interviewee, this also can lead to inconsistent answers. After the interviewee has provided an answer, summarizing and repeating back what you believe the person has said is a useful technique.

Example #23

Reconciling a Variety of Responses

Veronica complains about Luke, her supervisor, sexually harassing her. She states that the harassment occurred a year ago. When asked what made her complain now, Veronica says that earlier she was afraid that if she complained Luke would retaliate by demoting her or making her life difficult—but eventually, she simply could no longer tolerate the harassment.

Later in the interview, Veronica mentions that she just received a poor performance review from Luke. The investigator asks if that is why she has brought the complaint at this time and Veronica says perhaps, because now she sees that Luke is retaliating against her even though she did not complain when the harassment occurred.

Still later in the interview, the investigator asks what made Veronica come forward when she did and Veronica says she did not know the process for complaining until she spoke to her friend Kim about the harassment, and that Kim encouraged her to complain.

For many people, Veronica's three different reasons for the timing of her complaint would have the effect of undermining her credibility. Yet Veronica's reasons all can be reconciled. One difficult task in making a determination is deciding whether or not to accept explanations for inconsistent testimony. The poor performance review may be what Veronica is referring to when she says she could no longer tolerate the harassment. Perhaps Veronica then spoke to Kim, who encouraged her to complain.

In this situation the investigator will need more information about the connections between each of the events to evaluate whether Veronica's various reasons for bringing the complaint affect her credibility. Veronica may be accurately relaying some—but not all—of the details of what happened. Perhaps Luke did the acts she alleges but at the time his behavior was not unwelcome. Perhaps, after receiving a negative evaluation, Veronica has put a different spin on his actions.

Not being credible does not mean that someone is lying about everything. It may mean simply that he or she is leaving out important information that could put a different interpretation on the allegations.

Inherently Improbable

Some stories just don't make sense. They are inconsistent with the manner in which most people do things. Such stories are considered inherently improbable.

Example #24

The Far-Fetched Story

Fred is accused of having grabbed Sally's buttocks. When questioned, Fred turns red and says he saw a thread on the back of Sally's dress and thought she would want it removed so he took it off. The investigator asks how it was that Sally felt a squeeze, and Fred replies that he might have tripped when he went to remove the thread and had to grab on to Sally to keep from falling.

This story sounds awfully far-fetched. Sometimes the more questions you ask, the odder a story becomes! As the investigator you may rightfully conclude that one party's statement simply is not believable. But before you do so, let that party know you have concerns about his or her veracity and give him or her an opportunity to provide an explanation. Sometimes the explanation really clears up a credibility issue. At other times the witness digs him or herself further in the hole by providing even more outlandish explanations or by coming up with new, previously undisclosed facts that are clearly primarily self-serving.

Motive to Lie

The fact that a witness or party does or doesn't have a motive to lie will affect his or her credibility. This factor almost always weighs against the accused, which may make it seem a bit unfair. The reality is that the accused always has a motive to lie to protect himself or herself. On the other hand, the accuser usually does not have a motive to lie and, in fact, fabricated complaints are rare. They do happen, however—and complaints often are exaggerated. Moreover, witnesses often downplay their parts in an interaction that eventually became offensive. If the alleged harasser denies the allegations, determining whether the complainant has a motive to lie (such as a recent negative evaluation) is a necessary part of the investigation.

Questions that relate to potential motives to lie may make the person you are interviewing defensive. Ask these questions carefully. For example, to avoid having the interviewee "shut down" or become hostile, you can soften questions about performance problems or personality differences with the other party by explaining that to be thorough you need to understand the whole history of the situation. Being thorough also helps you anticipate responses the other party may have to the accusations. Sometimes simply being careful to use a nonjudgmental tone is enough to create a trusting atmosphere so that the interviewee will open up.

Declarations against Interest

Declarations against interest occur when a party admits to certain behavior that reflects poorly on him or her but denies other behavior. If certain acts are admitted but others are denied, the fact that the person admitted to certain behavior bolsters his or her credibility in relation to the behavior that is denied. Why would a person admit to certain acts and yet deny others? Another way to think about this is that a person who remembers only facts that help his or her case usually is not as credible as a witness whose memory is less selective.

Example #25

Forrest's Admission

Star has accused Forrest, her supervisor, of asking her out on a date and making a pass at her. She states that this occurred in January and that in October he asked her out again and when she refused he gave her a negative performance evaluation. Forrest admits that in January he asked Star out and that he made a pass at her, which he should not have done. He states that she slapped him and told him never to do that again. Forrest further states that he has not asked Star out since January and that her actions made him respect her wishes. Forrest states that he gave Star additional duties in June because he thought her work had been excellent, but it turned out that her performance on the new tasks was disappointing, which led to the October evaluation.

Here, Forrest's admission that he had asked Star out bolsters his credibility—especially given the detail he provided. He also has provided a reason why he wouldn't repeat the behavior and a possible reason for Star to be angry with him. His response puts Star's allegations in a new light.

In this case the investigator will need to go back to Star and assess the credibility of her responses to what Forrest had to say. For example, if she admits omitting information about the prior incident with Forrest (her slapping him), she should be questioned as to why she left this out.

Evaluating the Documents

In evaluating documents as evidence, consider the following points.

- Who prepared the document? A document prepared by an unrelated third party usually is more reliable than a document prepared by one of the parties to the dispute.
- Was the document prepared in the normal course of business? Such a document often is more reliable than one created after a party decides to bring a complaint or after the respondent is on notice of the complaint.
- When was the document prepared? A document prepared shortly after a conversation or event generally is given more consideration than one prepared later.
- Who had custody and control of the document? The chain of custody, which establishes whether someone else had an opportunity to create or change a document (or any piece of evidence) can be critical to the value the investigator should give the document.
- How consistent is the document with other documents prepared by the same person?

Checking Disciplinary History and Documents

Review personnel files or supervisory "desk files" of the complainant and the respondent in the process of making a determination. These files often contain background information on employee discipline, such as verbal or written warnings, that may be important in your evaluation of the circumstances of the relationships of people involved in the complaint. Retaliation claims, in particular, often involve charges that the victim has been singled out for supervisory attention when other co-workers have not been similarly monitored. The absence or presence of disciplinary action taken against employees other than the complainant helps establish whether the employer has been consistent in taking adverse actions.

Evaluating the Complainant's Reason and Timing

When a complaint is made weeks, months, or even years after the alleged behavior, examine the reason for the delay. The reason or reasons also may be a factor in determining disciplinary action.

Some complaints arise in the context of other disputes and work relationship problems. At times employees react to being disciplined by making a complaint of harassment or discrimination. This does not necessarily mean the complaint is invalid. Many victims of harassment do not complain, thinking that if they do complain it will jeopardize their jobs. Later, some of these employees may receive a poor evaluation and see that their jobs are threatened regardless of whether they complain. This realization may motivate some employees to come forward. On the other hand, some complainants bring untrue or exaggerated complaints primarily for the purpose of preserving their jobs. An important topic for most investigations will be why the complaint surfaced when it did. The timing of the complaint also may shed light on changes in the work relationship that you need to understand and factor in to your conclusions.

Making Your Findings

In the end you will need to make a determination whether each significant allegation occurred. Basically there are five distinct conclusions, or findings, that you can reach. Findings are discussed further in Chapter 10.

1. The allegations occurred essentially as alleged;
2. Some of the allegations occurred but some did not;
3. The incidents or events occurred as alleged but the complainant's interpretation of them was incorrect or unreasonable;
4. The allegations did not occur—the complainant fabricated them; or
5. No determination is possible.

Many investigators err by saying there is insufficient evidence to support the allegations without specifying whether they are concluding that the allegations were fabricated or that the available evidence was simply inconclusive. *Be specific as to what you are finding. Using language like that given above, make a finding for each element of the complaint.*

Another common mistake is to find that the complainant's allegations "are unsupported" because the respondent denied them and there is no direct corroboration. In many cases there will be enough evidence to make a determination based on a preponderance of the evidence. Be wary of taking the easy way out and failing to conclude whether the conduct occurred. This will not prove to be the easy way in the long run. Credibility determinations and the other investigative techniques discussed elsewhere in this book usually allow for a sound determination.

Some investigators find it helpful to make an analytical list of the allegations and put under each one a list of the facts that would support it and a list of facts that would tend to show the allegation did not take place. When all of the evidence has been listed, the investigator can more easily examine the significance of each fact. An illustration of an analytical list appears in Appendix A in the answer to the self-check for this chapter.

It is important to remember that many investigations will have multiple incidents or events that have been investigated. A proper investigation could find that one allegation is valid, another is not supported by the facts, and still a third resulted in no finding because of insufficient evidence or the inability to reconcile opposing perspectives.

Often you will find that conduct may have occurred that did not violate the employer's policy but rather reflected poor communication and personality conflicts. Because one type of complaint that gets immediate and serious attention is harassment, some employees will bring a "harassment" complaint when their true complaint lies elsewhere. Your findings may conclude that this is what happened. In general it is best for you to determine whether the alleged conduct occurred, *not* to determine whether the conduct violated the law. You or someone else designated by the employer (usually an HR manager or organizational leader) may make a determination as to whether there was a violation of the company's policies.

Chapter 8 Self-Check

This chapter has presented an overview of factors that can influence how you evaluate the evidence gathered in an investigation. To further your knowledge, consider the following scenario. Weigh the evidence and come to a determination. Compare your analysis with the suggestions provided in Appendix A.

Carolyn complains to HR about her supervisor, Jared. You are assigned to investigate.

Carolyn states that two weeks ago she took a day off because she was feeling ill. She states that by late morning she was feeling better so she decided to go out. While she was out she ran into Jared. Jared said he had a lunchtime business meeting with a prospective client, which is why he was dressed up in a suit and tie. After he left the office he received a call on his cell phone telling him that the client he was meeting with had an emergency and could not make it.

Carolyn states that Jared admonished her for not being at work in a joking way and suggested they have lunch. She agreed. During lunch he propositioned her. According to Carolyn, Jared said "I've always found you very attractive. Why don't you give me a chance?" Carolyn tells you she responded politely but firmly. She told Jared that she had no interest in dating him. According to Carolyn, Jared appeared to accept this but after they left the restaurant, and before they parted, he grabbed her and kissed her on the lips.

Carolyn states that there were no direct witnesses—there were people in the vicinity, but no one she knew. She also states that she wasn't going to complain to HR about this, and didn't want to do anything to hurt Jared. But yesterday Jared wrote her up for being absent again. In the write-up he mentioned her absence two weeks ago. She now fears that Jared is retaliating against her for refusing his advances.

Carolyn tells you that after the lunch she did call a close friend of hers at work, Adele. Adele does not work directly with Jared or Carolyn.

You interview Jared next. He is shocked at the allegation and denies having lunch with Carolyn on the day in question. He says he had lunch alone and then returned to the office. He also says he was afraid Carolyn might "pull something like this" because her performance and attendance have been marginal. She has called in sick on numerous occasions. When you inform him of the allegation about lunch he points out that if Carolyn was well enough to go out, she should have been at work. He thinks she saw the writing on the wall that she was headed for termination and is now trying to make herself "fire-proof." You ask Jared about his whereabouts on the day in question. He confirms that he was out of the office and had been planning to attend a business lunch that was canceled. You ask Jared how Carolyn would have known this information. He says that his assistant, David, was aware of his schedule and is a big gossip.

You interview David next. David confirms that Jared was planning to attend a business lunch on the day in question and that it was canceled after Jared left the office. David called Jared to let him know. Jared said he'd pick up lunch before coming back to work. David states he did not discuss Jared's schedule (or schedule changes) with Carolyn or anyone else at work.

You interview Adele next. She confirms that Carolyn called her the day of the lunch and was upset. Adele relates what Carolyn told her and it is consistent with what Carolyn told you. Adele states that were it not for her conversation with Carolyn, she would not have known Jared was downtown that day. They do not work together and she would have no reason to know this information.

What finding will you make in this case and why?

The Investigative Report

Concluding the investigation with a well-crafted written report helps ensure that each aspect of the investigation has been thoroughly examined and documented. Not every investigation ends in a written report. But most investigators agree that generally it is best to write a report. The advantages to concluding the investigation with a written report are summarized in Figure 17.

Figure 17. Advantages of a Written Report

A written report

- states the scope of the investigation,
- sets out the investigator's findings in clear language,
- forces the investigator to think through the evidence and issues, and
- makes an official record of what the investigator found and why.

Importance of the Written Report

The process of writing the report forces the investigator to take a hard look at the evidence. It is often not until this stage that you realize more evidence is needed, or that a certain witness wasn't asked a key question. While you are writing the report you still have the opportunity to go back and question that witness—and that is just what you should do. Writing the report also means that you must put into words the basis for your findings. This process may lead you to question—and perhaps change—some of your conclusions. Some investigators find that their efforts to produce a carefully worded report of findings provides them with the opportunity to systematically clarify and resolve conflicting and ambiguous information from the investigation.

Those investigators who do not provide a written report generally cite one of the following three reasons.

1. They are concerned about the time and expense involved in writing a formal report (and indeed, in some simple cases a written summary without a formal report may be appropriate).
2. They do not want a written record of their findings because if litigation ensues they prefer not to be pinned down to one version of what they determined.
3. They are concerned about one or both of the parties seeing the report, which might include evidence of witnesses who did not want to be disclosed or information from the complainant or respondent that he or she wanted to remain confidential.

The first concern is not a valid one. In all but the most simple of investigations, such as a case with only one minor allegation and no witnesses, the time and expense involved in writing a report is worth it to the employer. Some investigators find it difficult to write and may procrastinate or resist preparing the written report. Once you get started, it's not so onerous.

The second concern also should not prevent investigators from writing a report. It is best if the investigator is fully comfortable with his or her findings at the close of the investigation. If you begin to write an investigative report and find that you are uncomfortable with your findings, you may need to go back and gather more evidence. Writing the report can help you uncover the gaps in the information that can help you define your conclusions and prevent litigation. Putting off writing the report in the guise of concerns about future litigation is not recommended.

The last concern is a valid one. The written report may well end up in the hands of the parties—if not right away, then later if there is litigation. If the investigation is subject to the Fair Credit Reporting Act (see Chapter 4), the report may have to be disclosed to the respondent. The procedures required by some public agencies and in some union environments will likely generate wider than usual distribution of the report, with concomitant concerns about revealing the identity of witnesses and the contents of their statements.

If your investigation involves witnesses who have legitimate concerns about retaliation, their concerns should be taken into consideration as you write the report. You can summarize witness statements without naming the individuals and not attach the witness statements to the report. Or, you can delete the names of the witnesses if the report is provided to a party. In rare instances you may prefer not to prepare a written report. But it is better to find a way to protect witnesses and parties that allows you to complete your investigation with a written report.

The report, along with the investigator's notes and other documents, should be maintained in the appropriate filing location used by the employer for highly sensitive personnel documents. Typically, the investigation file will be kept separate form the personnel files of the employees involved. See Figure 14 in Chapter 6.

Contents of the Report

Organizing the report into different sections helps organize your thoughts and makes the report easier to read. A typical report will include three or four parts, as follows.

Preamble and Introduction

This introductory portion of the investigative report should contain information about

- who made the complaint;
- the date the complaint surfaced;
- who was named as the alleged harasser;
- the basic allegation(s);
- when the investigator began and concluded the investigation;
- other pertinent background about the complaint and investigation, including such details as who (or how many people) were interviewed, where the interviews took place, who (if anyone) was involved in coordination, and so forth; and
- additional (tangential) issues raised by witnesses or parties, depending on the course and scope of the investigation, because these issues may deserve a different form of management attention.

Findings of Fact and Factual Allegations

The findings of fact in the report should list all the allegations and the responses to those allegations. This part of the report can be organized by party (when there are multiple parties) or by allegation. Here you will detail what you were told by whom, but not evaluate or weigh the evidence. You need not include every fact you uncovered in the investigation, but all the facts that contributed to your conclusions and determinations should be listed.

Conclusions and Determinations

The determinations section is where you weigh the facts and come to conclusions as to what occurred. This part of the report is where you will state your determinations about whether or not contested facts happened in the manner alleged, in some other manner, or not at all. You also will explain your rationale for accepting or discounting conflicting witness accounts of important incidents. Most importantly, this is where you will state the basis for your determination.

The conclusions and determinations section surely is the most difficult part of the report to write because it is here that you are forced to back up your conclusions. As you draft this part of the report you may even find yourself reevaluating those conclusions. If you can't articulate why you have made certain findings, you may discover that they're the wrong findings! Although you may find this frustrating, in fact the report-writing process has accomplished an important goal by forcing you to clarify issues. Although you may have to rethink conclusions, this is just what is demanded and shows that you are indeed being thorough and fair.

Putting labels on behavior tends to make it harder for people to accept that the behavior occurred. It is better to conclude whether specific alleged conduct occurred than to write about the alleged conduct in terms of "sexual harassment" or "racial harassment" or some other broad label. Sometimes a report will word its conclusions to state that conduct occurred that "violated company policies" rather than state a determination that "harassment occurred." The investigator may do this in order to avoid conflict with the way the term "harassment" is defined under the law (see Chapter 2). For some investigations you will want to contact the employer's attorney for consultation about the best way to state your conclusions.

Recommendations

In most cases you will not be expected to make recommendations about remedial measures. In some cases the investigator will, after making determinations as to what took place, recommend certain actions or have input into what remedial actions will take place. Whether you will be called on to do this will depend on your position in the company. For outside investigators, whether you will have such input depends on the resources and point of view of the company's HR department and in-house counsel. From the standpoint of the employer, either approach is acceptable.

At times investigators will be asked to provide recommendations verbally rather than in writing. This also is acceptable. The types of remedial and disciplinary actions that employers may take are discussed in Chapter 10. A sample written report is provided in Appendix F.

Follow-up Letters

An investigation is not complete without formal follow-up to the parties. A letter from the authority who ordered the investigation is a highly recommended practice. Such letters provide an excellent opportunity to assert the organization leader's commitment to a harassment-free workplace and to place his or her authority squarely behind the employer's prohibition on retaliation. The letter should set forth the complaint and summarize the findings. Employer policies regarding harassment and, especially, the prohibition against retaliation, should be contained in or attached to the letter. A sample follow-up letter can be found at Appendix G.

If the report includes a finding for the complainant, the complainant should be informed that action is being taken. Many companies will not specify what the action is because of concerns for the respondent's privacy. Nonetheless, the message should come through that the complaint was taken seriously and appropriate action is being taken. If the investigation is inconclusive, or if there is a finding that the conduct did not occur, the complainant should be invited to bring forward additional evidence for consideration.

The letter to the respondent should include the findings, and for any specific finding of wrongdoing the actions, if any, that will be taken.

Chapter 9 Self-Check

This chapter has presented information that can help you organize the evidence and findings of your investigation into a written report. To further your knowledge, review the sample interviews in Appendix E. Based on these interviews, write (either in complete form or in outline form) a report of the investigation. Include a statement of facts, findings, and recommendations. After you have completed your report, compare it to the sample investigative report presented in Appendix F, which is based on the same set of facts.

CHAPTER 10

Remedial Actions

Possible Findings and Actions

Only after the investigation has resulted in a determination can the employer make a decision about what action to take. This decision usually is made by someone other than the investigator, but the investigator may have input into the decision and the action will, of course, depend on the determination made in the investigative report. As was discussed in Chapter 8, the investigation may result in various possible findings. The implications of these findings for remedial action are discussed below.

The Allegations Occurred

False complaints of harassment are rare. Therefore, a frequent determination in an investigation is that the allegations occurred, either in the manner they were alleged by the complainant or nearly so. A finding that the conduct occurred does *not* necessarily mean that actionable harassment has occurred as the term is defined under the law. It usually does mean that an employer policy has been violated. The violation could be a serious one, such as a sexual assault, or it could be relatively trivial, such as telling an offensive joke. The level of discipline imposed in the employer's action will depend on the circumstances of the incident and on other factors, including the routine discipline practices used in the organization.

Some of the Allegations Occurred but Others Did Not

A finding that some of the allegations occurred as alleged does not mean that all of the allegations occurred. Each allegation should be evaluated separately in the investigative report. The actions that the employer decides to take in response to the investigation should address only those allegations that were found to have occurred.

The Incident Occurred but the Complainant's Interpretation Was Incorrect or Unreasonable

This finding reflects the investigator's conclusion that the alleged behavior most likely did happen but that there is also no reason to believe that the respondent fabricated his or her denial. Rather, there was some sort of good-faith misunderstanding about what happened. Note that this finding asserts that an incident did occur but that there was a misunderstanding—not that an incident did not occur or that the complainant is making it up.

Example #26

The Case of the Misheard Word

Ralph has accused Cindy of calling him a "nigger." He states that they had been friends but he was so taken aback when Cindy called him this name that he has not been able to talk to her since the incident.

Cindy is shocked at the allegation. She states she finds the term "nigger" deeply offensive and would never use such a word. She also states that Ralph is stingy and when he purchased office supplies that she felt were of low quality in order to save a few pennies, she called him "niggardly." She says it did not occur to her that he would misunderstand that word and that she will not use the word "niggardly" in the future because of the confusion and hurt it can lead to.

When the investigator re-interviews Ralph, he says he thought Cindy called him a nigger" but that he is unfamiliar with the word "niggardly" and that it sounds like the same word to him.

Here, Ralph believed he was being called a racial epithet but, according to Cindy's credible testimony, this did not occur. In a case like this one, no adverse action would be taken against Cindy and none against Ralph for voicing the complaint—however the company would want both parties to resume a cooperative work relationship. The employer should make it clear that Ralph should feel free to make future complaints, if he has any. Reminding both parties about the company's policies is always a good idea.

The employer may also want to republish the policy or discuss it at a general meeting, being careful not to name names or put the complainant or respondent on the spot in any action taken. No record of the incident need be kept in the parties' personnel files; however, a record of the incident should be kept somewhere. If different employees should make similar complaints, what appears to have been a simple misunderstanding in one instance may actually be more than that.

If you determine that the complainant's concerns were based on a misunderstanding it may be useful also to determine the genesis of the misunderstanding. Was it reasonable? Did the respondent say or do something that could easily be misinterpreted? Would assistance with communication skills help prevent this kind of problem in the future? Did the complainant unreasonably interpret certain events? What actions might assist in preventing such an unreasonable interpretation in the future?

The Complainant Fabricated the Allegations

Although this situation is rare, if the company is confident with the level of proof that a complaint has been fabricated, disciplinary action should be taken against the complainant, consistent with how the employer would respond to other employees who breach trust. Employees should feel confident that their co-workers cannot make false claims without serious disciplinary action being taken.

Example #27

The Fabricated Allegation

Judy complains that her boss, Josh, propositioned her repeatedly. Josh states that he did ask Judy out once, but this was years ago, before he became her supervisor. He states that she refused at the time and that he hasn't said anything since. He also tells you he has been thinking of putting Judy on probation because of continued tardiness and poor work performance.

During the investigation Lisa, a co-worker of Judy's, tells you that Judy once confided in her that Josh had asked her out three years ago but Judy has never told her of any other incidents with Josh. Lisa states that Judy has said that if she's ever in trouble, she'll just bring a sexual harassment complaint against Josh by "warming up" the old request.

These facts would justify a finding that Judy had fabricated the complaint against Josh. The employer would want to discipline Judy in a manner that is consistent with how employees who are not honest would be disciplined. But if the employer considers terminating Judy, it would be best to consult with labor counsel before taking this action. There is a significant risk of Judy claiming the termination is retaliation for complaining about harassment.

Evidence Is Insufficient to Make a Determination

This finding is appropriately made when the investigator cannot resolve disputed accounts through the use of the techniques described throughout this book.

Example #28

Insufficient Evidence

Robert says that Claudia called him "Sambo." Claudia denies having said anything like this. There are no witnesses and there is no other evidence of wrongdoing. None of the employees in Claudia's unit have heard her use a derogatory term for African Americans. Both parties give credible statements and appear believable to the investigator.

In this situation no adverse action should be taken. But here the investigator has not determined there was a misunderstanding. There may indeed have been harassment, but there is inadequate proof. This situation must be closely monitored. The complainant should be made to feel comfortable coming forward with other information, if it arises. The respondent may receive a communication that clarifies appropriate and inappropriate comments and clarifies the consequences for the latter. Someone who has the skills to detect workplace problems should monitor the work environment.

In situations that require monitoring it's best to set up a "tickler" system to remind yourself to perform the check-in once or twice in the month or two following the conclusion of the investigation.

False Complaints of Harassment

In many organizations conflicts that do not involve harassment continue for long periods without attention on the part of managers or HR professionals. In such situations, employees may be tempted to add a label of harassment to their descriptions of work conflicts because, by doing so, they believe the problems will receive attention and action that would otherwise be unavailable.

Are such complaints of harassment false complaints? It depends. Frequently, after an investigation of a complaint has failed to establish that harassment occurred, investigators review what they have learned and conclude that a serious work relationship conflict did exist and precipitated the complaint. Such complaints generally fit into one of three categories as shown in Figure 18.

Figure 18. Types of False Complaints

1. The complainant sincerely believed that he or she was treated differently because of his or her membership in a protected class (see Chapter 2). The investigator determines that the action occurred but that there was no discriminatory treatment. The investigator here should not conclude that the complainant made a false complaint.

2. The complainant has failed to draw attention to his or her conflict by other means and so falsely describes the complaint as harassment. Here, if the allegations are legitimate but the casting of the allegations as harassment is not accurate, the employer should consider reeducating employees on the use of the harassment complaint mechanism and provide other avenues for employees to address other types of complaints.

3. The complainant is found to have falsified events or attempted to recruit other employees in claiming or being witnesses to harassment. This situation represents a serious problem and should be addressed through the use of appropriate measures.

Good HR practices, such as establishing grievance procedures and making counseling available from trained employee relations counselors, can help to meet employees' needs for resolution of work conflicts and work relationship problems. Such practices make it less likely that employees will resort to claiming harassment in order to draw attention to their problems.

How to Determine the Appropriate Action

Before any disciplinary action can be selected or invoked it is important to give the respondent the opportunity to be confronted with the evidence that has been compiled.

If you have made the determination that conduct occurred that violated the employer's policies, disciplinary action must follow. The following factors are ones that courts have looked to in determining whether the employer took appropriate action in response to instances of harassment.

Desirable actions are

- immediate;
- calculated to end the harassment;
- progressive (If the harassment does not stop, more serious action will then be taken.);
- consistent; and
- balanced against the seriousness of the offending conduct.

Factors that employers should consider in deciding what action to take include

- the seriousness of the underlying actions;
- whether there have been similar incidents by the same employee;
- whether the employee had a supervisory relationship to the complainant;
- the extent to which the respondent recognizes the wrongfulness of the behavior and has demonstrated a willingness and ability to refrain from future problematic behavior;
- the impact on the victim;
- what the complainant wants done (However, see below);
- whether a manager or supervisor knew about or condoned the behavior;
- the effects of the behavior on the work environment;
- how similar behavior has been treated in the past;
- whether the respondent had received training or had clear expectations for his or her behavior before the incident(s) occurred;
- the level of proof that guided the investigator in making the determinations (see below); and
- the difficulty the employer may encounter in monitoring compliance with prospective remedial measures.

Regarding the level of proof, "proof beyond a reasonable doubt" versus "proof by a preponderance of the evidence" should not affect the investigator's findings. But the level of proof may influence the employer's choice of disciplinary or remedial actions.

How a Complainant's Wishes May Influence Discipline

Complainants often have strong feelings as to what disciplinary action they want the employer to take. For a variety of reasons, an investigator will want to find out how the complainant feels about possible discipli-nary actions. The complainant's expressions of feeling may influence his or her credibility or help the investigator gain a better understanding of what occurred. For example, if a complainant wants an employee fired for what appears to have been a trivial act, the complainant may not be telling the whole story or may have an axe to grind with the respondent for another reason. Conversely, a complainant's desire for modest disci-plinary measures may bolster his or her credibility. The other reason a complainant's wishes come into play is that, if the harassment was signif-icant, the employer may have to protect the victim from further contact with the respondent. Keep in mind that knowing and complying with the complainant's wishes as to his or her security will likely be an important part of a satisfactory resolution.

The employer should never allow the complainant to believe that he or she is in a position to determine what disciplinary action will be taken. However in some circumstances, the complainant's wishes must be con-sidered.

For example, if a complainant, in good faith, would be uncomfortable with regular contact with the respondent, work schedule modifications may have to be made. In a small office, a termination may have to take place. Perhaps under the same circumstances but with a large employer, an employee found responsible for harassment could be given another chance. However the fact that the complainant and respondent would have to have day-to-day contact, coupled with the complainant's legiti-mate feelings, makes continued employment of the respondent impossible in a smaller company.

Disciplinary action never should be harsher than is reasonable and fair, regardless of the complainant's feelings. However, there will be times when more than one discipline would be appropriate and a harsher one is chosen to demonstrate the organization's commitment to its policy.

When a Good Performer Is Implicated

An employee who is implicated in a harassment complaint but who also is a good performer presents a difficult quandary for HR professionals and managers. The quandary can only be solved by carefully balancing two important objectives. On one side, pressure from various sources will exist to preserve the employment of productive workers who contribute to the good of the company. On the other side, the company will face increased liability if decisions about personnel actions are inconsistently applied.

A quick but risky action that many organizations take is to be lenient in recommending and implementing disciplinary action. Give careful thought to the implications of extraordinary actions under these circumstances. If future problems arise with the same individual, the organization will have to answer for its earlier decision. If a less productive employee commits a similar policy violation and does not receive similar consideration, a lawsuit may follow. Furthermore, the employer will surely be seen by some employees as being unfair.

Harsh measures are not always the answer, either. Employees who have earned respect because they are good performers usually get the benefit of a second chance when their behavior has violated company policies. Experienced managers are rightfully proud of their role in "salvaging" such employees by careful application of managerial attention and technique. When faced with the quandary of investigating and possibly disciplining a high performing employee for harassment, consider remedial measures such as one-on-one training and periodic monitoring of behavior.

Example #29

Indirect Evidence Implicates Ralph

Marcos accuses his supervisor, Ralph, of sexually assaulting him at work. There are no direct witnesses, but Marcos provides a credible statement and was seen after the incident by witnesses who described him as "disheveled and upset." Ralph denies the incident but during questioning Ralph changes his story as to what he was doing when the incident occurred. Also, Ralph was seen in the vicinity of the assault at the time it occurred. Based on this evidence, the investigator determines that the incident occurred.

When it comes time to determine discipline, the company is leery of terminating Ralph. He has worked there for ten years and has done excellent work. There have been no previous complaints. Thus, a decision is made to demote Ralph and move him to a different department.

In this situation the employer has had to balance its obligation to protect one employee—Marcos—with the loyalty it would normally extend to a good employee with a long service record—Ralph. Were there more direct evidence as to the accuracy of Marcos' complaint, the employer would be more confident in its factual conclusions and might therefore invoke more serious discipline on Ralph, regardless of his performance and service record. If there had been an eyewitness to the attack, more serious disciplinary action would certainly have been justified. Of course, even without direct evidence, there are times when investigators will be confident of making a finding that harassment occurred and serious disciplinary action (including termination) will be appropriate.

Before taking action, it is often a good idea for the employer to check with legal counsel, especially if the action will involve a termination. If you are contemplating taking action against an employee represented by a union, review the proposed action with the person who is most knowledgeable regarding past precedent and contract interpretation for disciplinary action. Collective bargaining agreements, a public employee's right to a fair hearing, and similar issues may restrict the choices of remedial action available to decision-makers.

Remember that both the respondent and the complainant may challenge the action taken. The respondent may state that it is too severe and the complainant may say it is not severe enough. If the respondent has been found to have engaged in harassment and is not terminated, future victims (if there are any) also can complain that the employer's action should have been more severe.

Someone with experience and authority regarding disciplinary matters must make the final decision as to what discipline to apply in any given situation. Most often this individual is not the investigator but rather the head of HR or an organizational executive.

Making the Victim Whole

If the employer makes a finding that harassment occurred, in addition to disciplining the respondent, the employer should look at whether actions can be taken to make the complainant "whole." Making someone whole is a legal concept that, in this context, means putting the victim back in the position he or she would be in had the harassment not occurred. For example, work time lost as a result of harassment can be compensated. In appropriate cases, counseling can be provided. If promotional opportunities were affected by the harassment, the employer should consider whether a promotion or other job benefit should now occur.

Addressing Issues Ancillary to the Complaint

During the investigation other matters may present themselves that require the employer's attention. Such ancillary issues may include complaints about matters unrelated to the investigation, determinations that a witness has been uncooperative or untruthful, and so forth. It is not unusual for the respondent, supervisors, and co-workers to make complaints about the complainant. These situations certainly should be addressed, but in a manner that separates the issue from the central complaint that was investigated.

Chapter 10 Self-Check

This chapter has given you an overview of the types of remedial actions an employer might consider following an investigation of workplace harassment. To further your knowledge, consider the following questions. Where applicable, answers to self-check questions have been provided in Appendix A. Other answers will depend on details particular to your organization.

1. On occasion, an investigation results in a determination that an incident occurred but the complainant's interpretation of what happened was the consequence of a good-faith misunderstanding. What elements would you expect to find in your investigation interviews with a complainant that might suggest a good-faith misunderstanding? In interviews with the respondent?

2. The range of disciplinary actions used to deal with employer policy violations often is described as "progressive discipline." A typical starting point in a progressive discipline situation is a verbal counseling session held with the employee. What types of violations of an employer's nonharassment policy would justify administering verbal counseling? Would you make a record of the verbal counseling? Why or why not?

CHAPTER 11

Post-Investigation Issues and Remedies

All too often employers believe that once a complaint has been investigated, a determination made, and action taken, the employer's duty to the complainant is over. It is understandable that employers believe this. The complaint has taken many hours away from other work and everyone involved is anxious to get back to their "real" work. Unfortunately, many serious problems can arise for the employer even after the complaint has been addressed. If these problems are ignored, a stellar response by the employer may turn into an inadequate one.

Many harassment lawsuits focus solely on retaliation that occurred after the complaint was dispensed with, even when the alleged harasser was terminated. For example, if an employee alleges that he or she was harassed and then demoted as a result of her complaint, even if you correctly conclude that he or she was not harassed, the employee could prevail on a retaliation claim if he or she could show that the demotion resulted *because* he or she had complained of harassment.

Remember, whether or not the alleged harassment occurred is not critical for a retaliation claim. In and of itself, retaliation is a form of discrimination that is actionable under the law. It is also not conduct that employers should allow both because of the duty to protect the complainant and because of the message it sends to other employees. Figure 19 gives examples of how retaliation may manifest itself in workplace settings.

Through the HR department, the employer should watch for any behavior that a complainant could experience as retaliation. Don't assume that the employee will come to you. Instead, the employer should take affirmative, documentable steps to assure that the work environment is not hostile or retaliatory. If the respondent will be supervised by someone new, the employer must balance the need for the new supervisor to monitor the

---

Figure 19. What Does Retaliation Look Like?

Retaliation against the complainants, respondents, or witnesses in harassment investigations is all too frequent and can take many forms. Because such retaliation is against the law, employers must take steps to prevent it. But what does retaliation look like? Behaviors typically associated with retaliation include

- ignoring or ostracizing the witnesses who support one side or the other in a dispute (who is no longer included in lunches, office discussions, and so forth);

- restricting an employee's access to training or advancement opportunities that otherwise would have been available (for example, an attorney who complains about sexual harassment later is determined to be too "overly sensitive" to handle a difficult client of her firm);

- spreading rumors about the employee, including the fact that he or she has brought a false claim of harassment, cost someone their job, or similar information;

- moving the complainant's office space; or

- demoting the employee because of work-related problems without first determining whether the problems related to the harassment.

---

respondent's behavior against the respondent's privacy rights. Someone in the organization must assure that there is no future harassing conduct and no retaliation takes place.

After the Investigation Is Over

Employers can take specific steps after the investigation has been completed to ensure that the company's follow-up and remedial actions are effective. For example, the organization can assign someone to

- meet with the parties;
- evaluate the effects the investigation has had on the workgroup;
- arrange for mediation;
- provide appropriate training; and
- follow up (in various ways).

The investigator may or may not be the one to do these tasks. It will depend on the investigator's skill and experience and also the rapport developed during the investigation. Usually it is better to bring in someone who does not have a "history" with the dispute. But the investigator's input into what should be done can be invaluable. This feedback should be passed on to someone with the authority to enact the suggestions.

Meeting with the Parties

Most investigations do not result in termination of employment for the respondent. This means that after most investigations, both parties remain working for the employer. Meeting individually with the complainant and respondent to conduct a debriefing after the investigation has been completed always is a good idea. The meeting can be conducted by someone in HR or a supervisor who's been in the loop of those who were informed about the investigation. The investigator also might conduct the meeting.

During the meeting, find out how the parties felt about the process. Listen to their feedback as to what was difficult and any suggestions they have to improve the process. Find out if they have concerns about what will happen from now on, and address those concerns. The respondent will likely have concerns about the effect the investigation will have on his or her job and the way he or she is viewed by the organization. The complainant may also have concerns about retaliation for having put the workgroup through a difficult period. It is natural for both the complainant and respondent to have a heightened sensitivity to proper workplace behavior for a period of time after the investigation concludes. Likewise, the employer may have expectations of the parties—especially the respondent—as to future behavior. Make sure that the employer's expectations are clearly expressed to the parties during the debriefing.

If either party quits after the investigation is complete, find out why and whether the employee's decision was related to the complaint or how the complaint was handled. It's never too late to try to fix something. If the only way you find out about retaliation is through an exit interview, do whatever is reasonable and proper to bring the employee back.

Some employee discipline unrelated to the complaint may have been held in abeyance until the investigation was completed. If such is the case, the disciplinary action(s) that need to be imposed toward the parties or witnesses should be considered in tandem with remedial measures having to do with the complaint.

Evaluating the Impact on the Workplace

The parties are not the only employees who feel the effects of a complaint and investigation. It is rare for co-workers not to know something about what is going on and equally rare for them not to have an opinion or a response. Often co-workers will have taken positions about the issues without having had access to all the facts. Indeed, you have tried very hard to keep those facts confidential—so how can the general members of the workgroup know what the company knows? It would be easier if co-workers didn't get involved, but they do—it's human nature. At times employees have become so involved that the development of employee factions has affected the productivity of the workplace. Collegiality is almost always compromised. It is up to the employer to determine how serious these problems are and to fashion ways to address them. Some suggestions are listed below.

Arranging for Mediation

Mediation is a nonadversarial way to resolve conflict. It is only successful if the parties to the mediation participate voluntarily. *Mediation should not be used as a substitute for investigating a complaint and taking action.* Mediation can be used after action has been taken to assist parties in repairing their relationship and moving toward the future. Mediation is a completely voluntary process. An employer may suggest it, but it should not be forced on anyone.

Efforts to provide mediation, such as arranging for an apology or a meeting between the complainant and the respondent, should be carefully planned and evaluated. The mediator should be a trained and neutral party. Do not attempt mediation if you are not confident of the mediator.

Example #30

Mending the Fractured Workgroup

Sheila and Bernadette both lodge a complaint against their co-worker, Don. They each provide similar information: They had been friends but Don pushed the boundaries of the friendship and ultimately sexually assaulted one of them and made crude statements to the other. Don had been disciplined before for sexual harassment. Few people in the workgroup know about this, however. Don had been transferred from a different office.

The group's supervisor, Peter, investigates and determines that the allegations were credible. He then makes the decision to fire Don. This decision leads to Sheila's and Bernadette's co-workers becoming angry with them. The co-workers feel that Sheila and Bernadette invited any harassment by being friendly with Don. The co-workers do not know the extent of the harassment. Nor do they know about Don's prior history of harassment. They do know that Don is a "nice guy with three kids" who is now out of a job. Thus, they dislike and distrust Sheila and Bernadette.

Peter hires a mediator-trainer to work with the entire workgroup. The consultant provides training about sexual harassment. She then spends an afternoon allowing the workgroup to air their feelings. Sheila and Bernadette initially do not want to share the details of the harassment. But when they hear the hostility and misconceptions expressed by members of their workgroup, they change their minds. Sheila, her voice cracking, talks about how Don betrayed her trust and how it made her feel. Bernadette describes being assaulted. The room is silent. In the silence, the group's opinion shifts from blame to sympathy toward Sheila and Bernadette and from sympathy to anger toward Don.

Mediation also has been used successfully in harassment situations when the respondent remained at work. Examples of situations where mediation might be a helpful approach include the following.

- A co-worker has crossed a line and been disciplined. The two employees agree to meet and discuss how they will interact in the future.

- An employee sues the employer for sexual harassment. After settling the case, the employee is going to return to work. The employer arranges for mediation sessions with the employee and the rest of the workgroup to help assure a smooth transition back to work.

- An employee claims that her supervisor harassed her. The investigation finds some inappropriate conduct but also determines there were misunderstandings and misinterpretations. The supervisor is angry and hurt that the employee lodged a complaint before speaking with him directly. The employee finds the supervisor "unapproachable." The employee and supervisor come from very different cultures. A mediator helps them sort out their communication so that they can continue working together by building mutual respect and an effective work relationship.

Provide Appropriate Training

A sexual harassment complaint provides an employer a good opportunity to evaluate the workforce's understanding of harassment. An employer's commitment to a harassment-free workplace will have been put under a microscope during the investigation. The investigation may reveal weaknesses in the knowledge of supervisors or employees. This "problem" can be turned into an opportunity by designing and implementing training that will address the deficiencies. The solution may be a wider distribution of existing training or a new or modified training program. Sometimes training can be done in separate sessions that focus on harassment at work. At other times they take place as part of regularly scheduled meetings.

Training also may occur on a one-on-one basis. Employers often include in the disciplinary action a requirement that an employee attend individual sessions addressing workplace harassment—especially if the employee is high in the chain of command.

Rarely is it appropriate for group training to include the discussion of a recently investigated complaint in the same organization or workgroup. Privacy concerns of the complainant, respondent, and witnesses would be unnecessarily compromised. If a recent complaint will be discussed, the decision to do so should be based on an intentional, carefully considered assessment of the need to do so, and it should be done only with the complainant's permission (see Example 30). Before discussing a specific harassment complaint in a group setting it is advisable to consult with legal counsel.

Follow-up

Regular follow-up with the parties and the workgroup is an important part of preventing future problems and retaliation. Follow-up efforts, such as meetings with the individual who complained, should happen frequently at first and can then taper off.

What Organizations Can Gain from a Harassment Investigation

Human resource professionals who have studied organizations have seen that while some organizations are able to learn from their mistakes, others tend to repeat mistakes. Organizations that are able to learn from mistakes and modify their behavior accordingly, are called "learning organizations." These types of organizations can gain important perspectives about their strengths and weaknesses from evaluating investigations. The complaint, including how and why it surfaced, provides critical information on what works and what doesn't work in the organization—and what changes would be useful.

Learning organizations take the opportunities they are given to learn from critical incidents. Often there is much to be learned from reviewing the information that came to light during a harassment investigation. Leaders can tap the investigator's experience to determine the effectiveness of their efforts to communicate nonharassment policies. The actions of supervisors and managers in relation to the incidents or the complaint can help gauge the need to increase training. HR can learn the pressures in workgroups regarding an employee who "doesn't fit in" and the viability of supervisory efforts to implement measures within a work group where individuals from diverse backgrounds join forces to work together.

Workplace Assessments

One way to reap the benefits of the learning that takes place in a harassment investigation is through post-investigation workplace assessments and team building. If a workgroup is not functioning well and it is difficult to determine how to fix the problem, the employer may consider hiring an outside consultant to do a workplace assessment. The assessment can look at harassment and the impact of a given complaint, but it also can be broader. Sometimes it takes someone from the outside to diagnose and treat a workplace problem. Team-building efforts can be developed to restore or establish a productive and cooperative work environment.

Conclusion

Despite well-coordinated prevention efforts and clear policies designed to promote a harassment-free workplace, employers cannot prevent all instances of harassment. Complaints of workplace harassment often are seen in a negative light, as divisive and disruptive. However a company's fair and thorough investigation is a necessary response that can ultimately assist in both clearing the air and improving working conditions. A well-handled investigation can set the stage for remedial actions that repair, to some extent, the damage done to the victim. A well-handled investigation also minimizes the damage done by rumors and innuendo within the workgroup. Employers that go beyond the investigation of a complaint to attempt to address the underlying problems that led to the complaint have made a true commitment to improving the work environment and eradicating harassment.

Chapter 11 Self-Check

This chapter has presented information designed to help you ease employees' transition back to normal operations following an investigation. To further your knowledge, consider the following questions. Where applicable, answers have been provided in Appendix A. Other answers will depend on details particular to your organization.

1. How has your organization responded to conflict between employees in the past? Think of three actions you could have taken to improve the response.

2. Consider the various methods for working with employees and workgroups after a complaint of harassment. Which techniques or approaches would succeed in your organization? Would you be able to implement appropriate interventions within a short amount of time? What would you need to do to be more prepared to implement workgroup interventions as needed?

Notes

1. Goleman, Daniel. *Emotional Intelligence: Why It Can Matter More than IQ*. New York: Bantam Books, 1995.

2. *Etter v. Veriflo Corp.*, 67 Cal. App. 4th 79 Cal. Rptr. 2d 33 (1988).

3. *Burlington Industries, Inc. v. Ellerth*, 118 S.Ct. 2257 (1998) and *Faragher v. City of Boca Raton*, 118 S.Ct. 2275 (1998).

4. *Meritor Savings Bank v. Vinson*, 477 U.S. 57 (1986).

5. *Oncale v. Sundowner Offshore Servs., Inc.*, 523 U.S. 75 (1998).

6. *Robinson v. Jacksonville Shipyards, Inc.*, (N.D. Fla.) 790 F.Supp. 1486 (1991).

7. *Weeks v. Baker & MacKenzie*, 63 Cal. App. 4th 1128 (1998).

8. *Kimzey v. Wal-Mart Stores, Inc.*, 107 F. 3d 568 (8th Cir. 1997).

9. *Coates v. Wal-Mart Stores, Inc.*, 976 P.2d 999 (N.M. 1999).

10. *Fuller v. City of Oakland*, 47 F. 3d 1522 (9th Cir. 1995).

11. *Ghebreselassie v. Coleman Sec. Service*, 829 F. 2d 892, *cert. denied*, 487 U.S. 1234 (9th Cir. 1987).

12. *Cuenca v. Safeway S.F. Employees Fed. Credit Union*, 180 Cal. App. 3d 985, 225 Cal. Rptr. 852 (1986).

13. *Miller v. City of West Columbia*, 322 S.C. 224, 471 S.W. 2d 683 (1996).

14. *Castleberry v. Boeing Co.*, 880 F. Supp. 1435 (D. Kan. 1995).

15. *Cotran v. Rollins Hudig Hall Intl., Inc.*, 17 Cal. 4th 93, 69 Cal. Rptr. 2d 900, 948 P.2d 412 (1998).

16. *Silva v. Lucky Stores, Inc.*, 65 Cal. App. 4th 256, 76 Cal. Rptr. 2d 382 (1998).

Answers to Self-Check Questions

Where the Self-Check is an exercise with no "answer," only the exercise is presented here.

Chapter 1 Self-Check

1. **What are the factors in your employer's workforce that would make the reporting of prohibited harassment more or less likely?**

   Harassment reporting is likely to be reduced in an organization where employees mistrust management or each other. Employees in these organizations frequently question the commitment of leaders to the principles of a harassment-free workplace. Other variables that may play a role in harassment reporting, or the lack thereof, include the balance in the management positions between people of both genders and the inclusion of racial and ethnic minorities in the executive ranks.

2. **What level of backing can you expect from your organization's operating units (for example, departments) in relation to providing the resources and leadership support that you will need to conduct an investigation? What can you do to increase the chances that operating units will back you?**

   Some organizations regard HR or the EEO function as an unresponsive bureaucracy. These organizations have more difficulty seeing a potentially positive outcome when HR or EEO investigates complaints. The best efforts to reverse the low expectations held in these organizations involve conducting training and disseminating information about the ways that HR or EEO policy enforcement can reduce risks of legal liability and increase productivity by helping workers create an environment that allows everyone's best efforts to come forward.

3. **What are the barriers in your organization to using emotional intelligence data to evaluate employee conflict? How can you overcome them?**

Emotional intelligence data and the insights gained from its use are not always given equal weight in comparison to the results of applying cognitive intelligence (the kind measured in traditional IQ tests). Some organizations, including those with a large proportion of trained engineers, scientists, or financial analysts in leadership positions, may significantly favor the "just the facts, ma'am" approach to resolving employee conflict—including, for example, harassment complaints. You often can make an impact in an organization like this by using your emotional intelligence and effectively articulating the value of your insights as an alternative to the perspective of others who are more inclined to favor an analytical approach.

Chapter 2 Self-Check

1. **Is harassment always unlawful? If not, what is the difference between harassment that violates the law and harassment that does not violate the law?**

Harassing behavior is not always unlawful. However, employers should prohibit any workplace conduct that might offend someone. This includes ethnic jokes, sexual jokes, teasing based on sex, race, age, ethnicity, and so forth. Much of this conduct, although serious, would not violate laws protecting employees from harassment. Hostile environment harassment that violates the law must be severe (such as a serious assault) or pervasive (repeated conduct over a period of time). *Quid pro quo* sexual harassment also violates the law. This refers to the type of harassment where a condition of employment (obtaining a raise or promotion) is contingent on providing sexual favors.

2. **How can employers protect themselves from legal liability for harassment? (Take a look at your own organization. Are you doing all you**

can to prevent harassment? Are your policies current and are employees aware of them? Are there steps you could take to improve your organization's prevention plan?)

Employers should take all reasonable steps to prevent harassment. This means promulgating anti-harassment policies, distributing these policies, making sure employees know about and understand the policies, providing training as needed (especially to supervisors and managers), and responding quickly and appropriately whenever the employer is on notice of harassment. Proper prevention and response to workplace harassment will not necessarily eliminate legal liability for every incident of harassment, but it will greatly reduce the risk of liability for most situations. You can conduct a harassment prevention audit of your own organization. Conducting such an audit on a regular basis and making improvements as needed greatly reduces your organization's risk of liability.

Chapter 3 Self-Check

1. **What factors have courts looked to in order to determine whether an investigation was reasonable?**

   Courts have looked at factors such as whether the investigator
   - was neutral and had been trained;
   - interviewed the alleged harasser and the victim and interviewed all pertinent witnesses;
   - reviewed all relevant documents;
   - documented the investigation and prepared a written report; and
   - communicated the findings in a confidential manner to the interested parties.

2. **If an employee complains about harassment and the employer investigates and finds that no harassment took place, could the employee file a lawsuit?**

   There is no separate legal claim for a failure to investigate or failure to adequately investigate harassment. However, in a legal action for harassment part of what the party bringing the action can claim is that there was either no investigation or an inadequate one. The fact that there was an adequate investigation could help shield the employer from liability in that lawsuit. On the other hand, if the party bringing the suit persuades the judge or jury the investigation was flawed, it could enhance both the likelihood of a verdict against the employer and the amount of the money awarded to the party.

Chapter 4 Self-Check

1. It is likely that, if you have worked in HR or EEO for your organization for an extended time, some past experience(s) with an employee will challenge your ability to be neutral should that employee appear as a complainant or respondent in an investigation. Keep in mind that the challenge could be either that you might be too critical of that person or too uncritical. What steps could you take to try to maintain your neutrality should an occasion like this arise?

    Past experiences with employees will not automatically impact your ability to be neutral or effective as an unbiased investigator. However, if you have had a negative experience with an employee, you should assess that experience. How strongly did you feel about the person? What about his or her honesty? Will any conclusions you came to based on that experience influence the way you perceive this person as you investigate the current complaint? When the past experience occurred, did you do anything to communicate your negative impressions to this person—or to anyone else who may have shared your perspective with the person? Similarly, if your past experiences with an employee have led to a very positive impression, ask yourself about your ability to recognize and anticipate the "halo effect" you may attribute to that person on the basis of your earlier experience(s).

2. Assume that you are asked to investigate a complaint involving allegations about the behavior of top executives in your organization. Do you think you would be suitable to do this? If not, why not? How can you overcome those concerns?"

    Evaluate how the difference between your status in the organization and the respective status of the complainant(s), respondent(s), and witnesses may affect your role as an investigator. You will have to interview these people and evaluate their responses. If you have scant experience with high-ranking executives, it may be possible for a party or witness to intimidate you by implying that you do not and cannot understand all the influences that she or he is required to keep in mind when she or he performs work. Be mindful also that your witnesses may perceive a certain distance if your level in the hierarchy is substantially higher than theirs. In either situation it may be best for you to work with another person so that the investigative team, considered as a unit, minimizes the impact of organizational status differences.

Chapter 5 Self-Check

Here are some sample questions an investigator could ask Jamal.

1. Approximately when did you convert to Islam?

2. How did people with whom you work become aware of your conversion?

3. With whom among your co-workers were you friends at work or outside of work before you converted? With whom were you friends after you converted?

4. Does George assign work to you? What other supervisory functions, if any, does George have?

5. Had you and George had discussions about religion or religious practices before the night you mentioned in your complaint?

6. What exactly did you say and how did George respond on the night when you told him you weren't going to celebrate the Christmas holiday?

7. Who are the co-workers that eat lunch at the same time and in the same area as you?

8. Did you or the co-workers make fun of anyone else during lunch? If so, provide details.

9. What food items do you normally have in your lunch? Are any of them related to religious practices unique to Islam?

10. Who brought up the subject about wearing turbans, and what did they say in relation to being a Muslim?

11. What, if anything, did you say when your co-workers talked about your food? When they made the comment about turbans?

12. What would you like to see changed in the workgroup as a result of making your complaint?

13. Please show me copies of the pictures you put up in your area of the tool room. Who are the other employees who have put up pictures in the tool room? Where are their workstations in relation to yours?

14. Have any of your co-workers also had their pictures taken down?

15. Was the schedule changed as a result of the discussion you had with George about not celebrating Christmas? If it was changed, were you disadvantaged in any way?

Chapter 6 Self-Check

For additional practice with note taking and preparing statements, interview friends or co-workers about something important that happened between them and a friend or neighbor or about something unusual that they witnessed. Ask them to choose a topic with which you would not normally be involved. Take notes and have them review your notes for accuracy. Then draft statements, in their words, about the event. Get their honest feedback as to the accuracy of the statements, both factually and in terms of the flavor of what they were conveying. Did you miss something important? Did you put your own gloss on the topic? Try this exercise with a few different people until you receive consistent feedback that your draft statements accurately reflect what they have said.

Chapter 7 Self-Check

1. Complainant: "Everyone knows that nothing is going to change around here, so why bother with asking me all these questions?"

Your answer may include the following points: Empathize with the complainant's frustration but restate the purpose of the interview. Point out that you must collect all information so that careful analysis can be done of any behavior that may have violated company policies.

2. Complainant: "I don't know why I should have to talk to you. I've told managers about this problem already and all that happened is that I was called a chronic complainer and a bitch."

    Your answer may include the following points: Respond to the complainant's concern that managers haven't seemed responsive by explaining that you will be asking for all the details—not only about what happened, but also about the times the complainant told a manager or supervisor and what that person did or said. Restate the prohibition against retaliation (the complainant will be protected from any reaction, such as name-calling, that happens as a result of participating in the investigation).

3. Respondent: "I want to know right now everything that has been said about me, who said it, and all the details of what I supposedly did that was so wrong. My attorney told me not to answer questions until I have this information."

    Your answer may include the following points: Explain that in due course you will cover all the relevant details in the complaint, but for now you need to gather some background information so you can gain an understanding of the respondent's role and his or her perspective. Reassure the respondent that, before the interview concludes, he or she will know all the details and will have a chance to explain his or her side of the story.

4. Respondent: "(Complainant) has been a troublemaker for years. I'm the first manager that has stood up to it and challenged him (or her). Now you are accusing me of harassment because I did my job."

    Your answer may include the following points: Explain that the respondent's job responsibilities and his or her management of the complainant is a central focus of the investigation. State that you will be giving the respondent the chance to fully explain the circumstances that led to his or her need to exercise managerial authority, including whatever steps he or she took to be fair to the complainant.

5. Witness: "HR is anything but a neutral party around here. Before I say anything, I want to know who you are going to discuss my interview with."

    Your answer may include the following points: Explain that it is very important for the investigation to be neutral and that you have taken and will take all steps to ensure confidentiality to the maximum extent possible. Ask the witness about experiences that he or she has had with HR that led to the conclusion that HR will not be neutral. If the witness continues to be mistrustful, suspend the interview and seek advice from an HR executive or legal counsel as to how to proceed.

6. Witness: "Two years ago we had an investigation and three of the people who participated got laid off and one person was transferred against his will. What assurances can you give me that I won't be punished in a similar way for answering your questions?"

    Your answer may include the following points: Ask the witness to give you the names of the people who participated in the earlier investigation and what led the witness to believe that their layoffs or transfers were connected to the investigation. Reiterate the employer's policy regarding nonretaliation and invite the witness to contact you if he or she later becomes concerned that his or her role in the investigation has led to any problem with his or her employment status.

Chapter 8 Self-Check

Analysis

This is your classic "he said, she said" situation. No direct witness can corroborate the facts and the facts are relatively egregious. There is an indirect witness, Adele. This weighs in Carolyn's favor, especially because Carolyn spoke to Adele before she received a write-up. On the other hand, Adele is Carolyn's good friend and is not entirely without bias. Furthermore, Carolyn may have been anticipating the write-up. If Carolyn were very devious, she could have set this situation up by informing Adele of harassment the day she took off and then went out. Jared has ascribed to Carolyn a motive to lie, and the fact that she complained after receiving a write-up undermines her credibility to some extent.

However, even without Adele, there is evidence that enhances Carolyn's credibility. Carolyn complained about an incident that occurred off premises at a time that Jared was off premises. She was not at work that day. If she did not see Jared, how would she have known where he was? Perhaps she knew he had plans to meet with a client. If so, how would she know the plans were canceled? It would have been foolish to make up a story about a lunch with Jared when he was having lunch with a client (an easily verifiable fact). Perhaps she learned the lunch was canceled when she returned to work the next day. But this would not explain Carolyn telling Adele—that evening—about the lunch. Nor would it explain how Carolyn would know what Jared was wearing. The investigator here might want to go back and find out if Carolyn could accurately describe what Jared was wearing. This is something she would have no way of knowing unless she saw him (or there is a conspiracy going on between Carolyn and other employees—a highly unlikely situation).

For the above reasons, Carolyn would be found to be more credible than Jared. However, because the determination would be made based on circumstantial rather than direct evidence, the employer might be leery of terminating Jared (unless there were previous incidents).

If Jared admits to having had lunch with Carolyn (or perhaps to running into her but not having lunch) but he denied the comments and kiss, the determination will be much harder. Adele's statement would weigh in Carolyn's favor, but the write-up would weigh against her. Perhaps Jared's "joking" statement about Carolyn not coming to work tipped her off to a problem. Indeed, she should have gone in to work. Running into her supervisor under these circumstances was not a desirable situation from her point of view.

In balance, the fact that Carolyn spoke to Adele the same day of the incident carries greater weight than her motive to lie. As stated above, only a very devious person would set this kind of situation up by lying to a friend. However, it would be important to examine both Carolyn's and Adele's statements. Were they consistent? Did they appear genuine and not coached? It also would be important to ask Jared what he said about Carolyn missing work. If he made it clear to Carolyn that he was annoyed, this information would tip the balance toward his side and make the credibility determination far more difficult.

Analytical List

Carolyn's Version of Events

Credible	Not Credible
Reported incident to friend contemporaneously	Reported incident to HR two weeks after incident
Knew Jared was out of the office and in a suit and tie despite the fact that she did not work that day	Fear of discipline for attendance problems is a motive to lie
Provided a detailed account—making this story up would exhibit an unusual level of deviousness	

Jared's Version of Events

Credible	Not Credible
Not known by other witnesses to be dishonest	Denied even seeing Carolyn, despite the fact that Carolyn knew he was out of the office and what he was wearing

---

Chapter 9 Self-Check

Review the sample interviews in Appendix E. Based on these interviews, write (either in complete form or in outline form) a report of the investigation. Include a statement of facts, findings, and recommendations. After you have completed your report, compare it to the sample investigative report presented in Appendix F, which is based on the same set of facts.

Chapter 10 Self-Check

1. On occasion, an investigation results in a determination that an incident occurred but the complainant's interpretation of what happened was the consequence of a good-faith misunderstanding. What elements would you expect to find in your investigation interviews with a complainant that might suggest a good-faith misunderstanding? In interviews with the respondent?

A good-faith misunderstanding very likely will reveal itself in response to specific interview questions where the facts are consistently described by witnesses, including the complainant and respondent. You learn, however, that the context of the situation is seen very differently by the complainant and the respondent. Complainants may refer to previous difficult interaction(s) with the respondent and, when "one more thing" happened, the complainant thought that it was simply a continuation of the earlier pattern. Respondents may explain that, in the past, they had made similar remarks or gestures that were met with apparent acceptance or even welcomed by the complainant. In the respondent's estimation, the incident that gave rise to the complaint was no different than the earlier situations—but, inexplicably, the complainant reacted much differently.

2. The range of disciplinary actions used to deal with employer policy violations often is described as "progressive discipline." A typical starting point in a progressive discipline situation is a verbal counseling session held with the employee. What types of violations of an employer's nonharassment policy would justify administering verbal counseling? Would you make a record of the verbal counseling? Why or why not?

A good-faith misunderstanding that has not been preceded by more serious offensive behavior probably is a situation for which verbal counseling can be the best form of disciplinary action. Other factors discussed in the text, including the relative absence of serious harassment and the respondent's willingness to use the complaint as a learning opportunity, would make verbal counseling a good disciplinary choice. The verbal counseling should, however, be documented (provided that there is no prohibition to do so in any applicable employer policies, civil service rules, or a collective bargaining agreement). Documentation of the verbal counseling establishes a record that may later become important should questions be raised about the enforcement efforts pursuant to an employer's nonharassment policy. In some circumstances the best HR practice will be to maintain the documentary record of the verbal counseling in the investigation file instead of the personnel file of the respondent.

Chapter 11 Self-Check

1. How has your organization responded to conflict between employees in the past? Think of three actions you could have taken to improve the response.

   Answers will vary. Knowing how your organization responds to conflict can help you prepare for the fallout of a harassment investigation. Is there a reasonable need for detailed information? If so, how will you communicate what has happened without breaching confidentiality? Do employees tend to form factions? If so, what activities will help bring employees back together again? Plan to anticipate these problems and be ready with solutions so that you can weather a harassment investigation with grace.

2. Consider the various methods for working with employees and workgroups after a complaint of harassment. Which techniques or approaches would succeed in your organization? Would you be able to implement appropriate interventions within a short amount of time? What would you need to do to be more prepared to implement workgroup interventions as needed?

   Answers will vary. If you have tried to use mediation to resolve conflicts in your organization, you may have mediators available who can be called on in the aftermath of a harassment investigation. If not, look to developing these resources now. You also can review your organization's current training program. The more employees know about your company's anti-harassment policies, the more likely they will be "on board" should you have to investigate a complaint.

Massachusetts Model Policy

Some states provide model harassment policies; check with the appropriate office in your own state. Here is the Massachusetts policy.

**Commonwealth of Massachusetts Commission
Against Discrimination
Model Sexual Harassment Policy MCAD Policy 96–2**

Sexual Harassment Policy of [name of employer]

I. Introduction

It is the goal of [name of employer] to promote a workplace that is free of sexual harassment. Sexual harassment of employees occurring in the workplace or in other settings in which employees may find themselves in connection with their employment is unlawful and will not be tolerated by this organization. Further, any retaliation against an individual who has complained about sexual harassment or retaliation against individuals for cooperating with an investigation of a sexual harassment complaint is similarly unlawful and will not be tolerated. To achieve our goal of providing a workplace free from sexual harassment, the conduct that is described in this policy will not be tolerated and we have provided a procedure by which inappropriate conduct will be dealt with, if encountered by employees.

Because [name of employer] takes allegations of sexual harassment seriously, we will respond promptly to complaints of sexual harassment and where it is determined that such inappropriate conduct has occurred, we will act promptly to eliminate the conduct and impose such corrective action as is necessary, including disciplinary action where appropriate.

Please note that while this policy sets forth our goals of promoting a workplace that is free of sexual harassment, the policy is not designed or intended to limit our authority to discipline or take remedial action for workplace conduct which we deem unacceptable, regardless of whether that conduct satisfies the definition of sexual harassment.

II. Definition of Sexual Harassment

In Massachusetts, the legal definition for sexual harassment is this: "sexual harassment" means sexual advances, requests for sexual favors, and verbal or physical conduct of a sexual nature when

(a) submission to or rejection of such advances, requests or conduct is made either explicitly or implicitly a term or condition of employment or as a basis for employment decisions; or

(b) such advances, requests or conduct have the purpose or effect of unreasonably interfering with an individual's work performance by creating an intimidating, hostile, humiliating or sexually offensive work environment.

Under these definitions, direct or implied requests by a supervisor for sexual favors in exchange for actual or promised job benefits such as favorable reviews, salary increases, promotions, increased benefits, or continued employment constitutes sexual harassment.

The legal definition of sexual harassment is broad and in addition to the above examples, other sexually oriented conduct, whether it is intended or not, that is unwelcome and has the effect of creating a workplace environment that is hostile, offensive, intimidating, or humiliating to male or female workers may also constitute sexual harassment.

While it is not possible to list all those additional circumstances that may constitute sexual harassment, the following are some examples of conduct which if unwelcome, may constitute sexual harassment depending upon the totality of the circumstances, including the severity of the conduct and its pervasiveness:

- Unwelcome sexual advances, whether they involve physical touching or not;
- Sexual epithets, jokes, written or oral references to sexual conduct, gossip regarding one's sex life; comment on an individual's body, comment about an individual's sexual activity, deficiencies, or prowess;

- Displaying sexually suggestive objects, pictures, or cartoons;
- Unwelcome leering, whistling, brushing against the body, sexual gestures, suggestive or insulting comments;
- Inquiries into one's sexual experiences; and
- Discussion of one's sexual activities.

All employees should take special note that, as stated above, retaliation against an individual who has complained about sexual harassment, and retaliation against individuals for cooperating with an investigation of a sexual harassment complaint is unlawful and will not be tolerated by this organization.

III. Complaints of Sexual Harassment

If any of our employees believes that he or she has been subjected to sexual harassment, the employee has the right to file a complaint with our organization. This may be done in writing or orally.

If you would like to file a complaint you may do so by contacting [name, address and telephone number of the appropriate individual to whom complaints should be addressed. Such individuals may include human resources director, manager, legal counsel to organization or other appropriate supervisory person]. [This person] [These persons) [is/are] also available to discuss any concerns you may have and to provide information to you about our policy on sexual harassment and our complaint process.

IV. Sexual Harassment Investigation

When we receive the complaint we will promptly investigate the allegation in a fair and expeditious manner. The investigation will be conducted in such a way as to maintain confidentiality to the extent practicable under the circumstances. Our investigation will include a private interview with the person filing the complaint and with witnesses. We will also interview the person alleged to have committed sexual harassment. When we have completed our investigation, we will, to the extent appropriate inform the person filing the complaint and the person alleged to have committed the conduct of the results of that investigation.

If it is determined that inappropriate conduct has occurred, we will act promptly to eliminate the offending conduct, and where it is appropriate we will also impose disciplinary action.

V. Disciplinary Action

If it is determined that inappropriate conduct has been committed by one of our employees, we will take such action as is appropriate under the circumstances. Such action may range from counseling to termination from employment, and may include such other forms of disciplinary action as we deem appropriate under the circumstances.

VI. State and Federal Remedies

In addition to the above, if you believe you have been subjected to sexual harassment, you may file a formal complaint with either or both of the government agencies set forth below. Using our complaint process does not prohibit you from filing a complaint with these agencies. Each of the agencies has a short time period for filing a claim (EEOC—180 days; MCAD—six months).

1. The United States Equal Employment Opportunity Commission
    One Congress Street
    Boston, MA 02114
    (617) 565-3200

2. The Massachusetts Commission Against Discrimination (MCAD)

    Boston Office: **Springfield Office:**
    One Ashburton Place   424 Dwight Street
    Boston, MA 02108   Springfield, MA 01103
    (617) 727-3990   (413) 739-2145

    Worcester Office:
    22 Front Street
    P.O. Box 8038
    Worcester, MA 01641
    (508) 799-6379

The MCAD has revised its governing regulations (804 CMR 1.01) as of January 1st, 1999.

The Massachusetts Commission Against Discrimination
Copyright © 1998, http://www.state.ma.us/. Used with permission.

Sample Witness Statements

Statement of Allen (Complainant)

Taken by: [Investigator]
Date: [Month, Day, Year]

June XX, XXXX, I entered the office area at the First Street Yard. Bob H. was in his office and Terri was at her desk with her window open. Bob C. was in the office when I arrived but he was on the phone over at the corner desk.

I told Bob H. never to call me a "gimp" again. I also said that I was offended when he made fun of me and others, including Bob C. Bob H. has called me a "gimp," "wimp," "whiner," and "cry baby" more times than I can remember. Every time there are other workers around, Bob H. starts calling me names to get people laughing. Many times I heard Bob H. teasing Bob C. about taking periodic insulin injections because of Bob C.'s diabetes. I explained that my mother had diabetes and I knew firsthand how difficult a disease it is to get under control without the taunts of co-workers.

Terri said, "You're a chicken-shit wimp, you can't even take a little teasing but you can sure dish it out. All you are really interested in is kissing Bob C.'s ass because he rotates to your area as foreman next month." I didn't say anything to Terri and turned to walk out. I was disgusted because this was one more instance of Terri using profanity to put someone else down. I don't recall that I said anything more at the time.

The foregoing is a true and correct statement.

Signed: _____

Statement of Bob H. (Respondent #1)

Taken by: [Investigator]
Date: [Month, Day, Year]

June XX, XXXX, I was working in the office area at the First Street Yard. Terri was at her desk and she was helping me cover for the dispatcher, who was on a lunch break. Allen came into the office and started cussing me out. He said something like, "You're nothing but a f'ing troublemaker." Terri told him not to talk like that. I have heard Allen use profanity at work several times and, if Terri is there, she always calls him on it.

Terri and Allen started arguing and both of them got upset. I don't remember anything specifically that was said but I know that they were loud and I tried to calm them down by saying, "Let it go."

I never heard Terri say any profanity to Allen. Terri and I are friends outside the office but she is always strictly professional when she is at work. I didn't hear any comments made by Terri about Bob "kissing ass" or anything else that would be personally disrespectful.

Sometimes the guys in the yard joke around and call each other nicknames. My nickname is "the Wop." I don't get offended when people use my nickname because I know it's all in fun. Sometimes I tease other guys but I never do anything to hurt someone. If a guy tells me to knock it off, I will do so right away. Allen has the nickname of "Wimpy" because he always eats hamburgers, like the cartoon character in Popeye. Everyone, including me, calls him "Wimpy" when the guys are joking around.

I never said anything about Allen's disability nor did I make fun of him. He sometimes makes fun of himself, saying that he is a "cripple" and a "retard." Bob C. also teases me and calls me and others by our nicknames. Bob C.'s nickname is "Sugar" because he has diabetes.

If anyone, including Allen, had ever told me that they were offended by the joking around we do, I would stop right away and get the other guys to stop also.

The foregoing is a true and correct statement.

Signed: _____

Statement of Terri (Respondent #2)

Taken by: [Investigator]
Date: [Month, Day, Year]

June XX, XXXX, I was verbally abused by Allen. He came in after lunch and I thought he had been drinking because I saw that his eyes were red and his speech was slurred. He ripped into Bob H. about something but I couldn't understand what he was complaining about. I tried to get him to calm down but he started yelling at me, too.

Allen called Bob H. an "f'ing ass." When he said that for the second or third time, I told him not to talk that way or I would make a report. He walked right over to me and I felt that he was going to strike me. I backed up so my desk was between me and Allen and picked up the phone. He was real belligerent. When I started to dial the phone, he turned and left the office.

I was extremely upset and talked to Bob H. about what to do. Bob C. was in the office too but he never said anything even though, as a foreman, he is supposed to keep things under control. Bob H. told me to let things die down and get ready to make a report if anything like this happens again.

I never said anything to Allen about him "kissing ass" or anything else like that. I don't use that language and don't allow people to talk that way around me.

I never heard Bob H. say anything about Allen's bad leg. Allen has called himself a "cripple" and many people tease Bob C. by calling him "Sugar" because he is a diabetic. Bob C. always jokes around, so I never understood that Bob C. was offended by the teasing.

The foregoing is a true and correct statement.

Signed:_____

Statement of Bob C. (Witness)

Taken by: [Investigator]
Date: [Month, Day, Year]

June XX, XXXX, I stopped by the office at the First Street Yard to use the phone. Bob H. and Terri were in the office when I arrived; Allen came in a short time later. I started my phone call and didn't hear what was being said in any other part of the room.

I soon became aware that people were getting upset because I overheard all three people using loud voices like they were arguing. I remember that profanity was being used because I didn't want the person I was talking on the phone to hear it so I put my hand over the mouthpiece when I wasn't talking. I don't remember what profane words were used or who said them. Once I put the phone down when my call was done, I heard Terri tell Allen that he was an "ass kisser." I didn't hear anything that Allen said back to Terri or Bob H. because the phone rang and I answered a call from a ticket agent about a spill that needed to be cleaned up. I left right away to help the ticket agent.

I have had experience with my co-workers teasing me about taking insulin shots for my diabetes. I never took any offense to the teasing and it doesn't bother me. I couldn't say all the names of the people who have teased me because almost everyone does, except for Allen. His Mom had diabetes and we have talked about all the things you need to do.

The foregoing is a true and correct statement.

Signed: _____

Sample Introductions to Investigative Interviews

The same approach and similar information should be given in all interviews. However, the statements to the complainant, respondent, and witnesses should be tailored as shown.

Hello, I'm Rebecca from HR.

To Complainant: I'm here to investigate your allegation of a possible violation of our harassment policy.

To Respondent: I'm here to investigate an allegation that you violated our harassment policy. I want to get a complete response from you.

To Witness: I'm here to investigate an allegation of a possible violation of our harassment policy. You are not alleged to have done anything wrong; however, you may have some relevant information about the allegation.

Before we start I want to explain my role and go over how we will proceed.

First of all, I am here as a neutral party to gather information. I will be asking you questions. I'll try not to make you uncomfortable, but it's important for me to get as much information as possible. I'll be taking notes as we talk, and when we're done I'll make the notes into a statement for you to check for accuracy and sign.

I want to keep this matter as confidential as possible, so I am asking that you not discuss this matter—either what you've told me or what I've asked you—with anyone who works for this company. Can you agree to that?

After I've spoken to you, I'll interview other witnesses and come to a determination. I'll do this as quickly as possible. Completing all the interviews will probably take about a week, and if it will take longer I'll let you know. You also can call me if you have questions or concerns along the way.

To Complainant: You have a right not to be retaliated against for bringing a complaint. If you experience anything you would consider to be retaliation, please tell me right away.

To Respondent: You have a right to know and respond to each allegation but not to know who made the complaint. I want to emphasize that you have a duty not to retaliate against anyone for bringing a complaint or participating in an investigation. Can you agree to that?

To Witness: Also, although I know it's difficult, please try not to speculate about what the allegations are or who brought the complaint. Can you agree to that? I also want to tell you that you have a right not to be retaliated against for participating in an investigation, and a duty not to retaliate against anyone else. If you experience anything you would consider to be retaliation, please tell me right away.

Do you have any questions or concerns before we start?

Sample Interviews, Notes, and Statements

The following abbreviated interviews of a complainant, respondent, and witness are based on a hypothetical complaint by Sarah concerning her co-worker, Mitchell. In a real interview more time would be spent on background information and on getting further details of the allegations. These sample interviews are intended only to give a sense of what the question-and-answer process is like. For practice on note taking, try writing notes as you read the interviews, and then compare your notes to those on the pages that follow the mock interviews. For practice on statement writing, draft a brief statement for each person interviewed and then compare your draft to the samples provided after the notes.

Points to Notice in the Interviews

As you read these sample interviews, notice the use of open-ended questions and the use of where, what, when, and who. When a question is not answered with specificity, notice how the investigator returns later to get more specifics. Also notice how the investigator deals with tough questions and nonresponsive answers.

Sample Interview with the Complainant

Investigator: Hi Sarah, I'm Jackson from HR. I'm here to investigate your complaint about Mitchell. I'm here as a neutral party to do fact-finding. I'll be taking notes for you to review and sign. I'm going to keep this matter as confidential as possible and I need your cooperation in this.

Sarah: Well, I already told my boyfriend, Steve.

Investigator: That's fine, assuming Steve doesn't work for ABC Corporation. But I don't want you to speak to anyone who works here. Okay?

Sarah: Okay.

Investigator: I also want you to know that it's against company policy and the law to retaliate against someone for bringing a complaint of harassment. Please let me know if you experience anything you feel is retaliation. Okay?

Sarah: Okay.

Investigator: Great! Are you comfortable going forward and telling me what happened?

Sarah: Yeah, I suppose. Mitchell came on to me.

Investigator: When did this happen?

Sarah: Yesterday.

Investigator: What time?

Sarah: About eight-thirty, just after I got to work.

Investigator: Where were you when this happened?

Sarah: The break room.

Investigator: Was anyone else there?

Sarah: Not at first, but Henry came in.

Investigator: Do you think Henry heard anything?

Sarah: I don't know.

Investigator: Have you spoken to Henry about this?

Sarah: No.

Investigator: Have you spoken to anyone other than your boyfriend about what happened?

Sarah: No—well, except my supervisor, Miguel.

Investigator: Sarah, can you tell me exactly what Mitchell said that bothered you?

Sarah: Well, he made a comment about my body. He said I had such a great body; he wanted to see what it could do. It gave me the creeps.

Investigator: Where was he when he said this?

Sarah: Like I said, it was in the break room.

Investigator: Can you tell me where you both were standing?

Sarah: I was at the coffee machine and Mitchell walked up to me while I was making coffee. He stood behind me and said this in my right ear.

Investigator: Did you respond?

Sarah: No, I just looked at him and walked out. I came back later for my coffee.

Investigator: Has Mitchell ever done anything else to make you feel uncomfortable?

Sarah: No.

Investigator: Do you know of anyone else whom he might have made feel uncomfortable?

Sarah: No.

Investigator: Can you think of any reason Mitchell would do this?

Sarah: How would I know?

Investigator: Is there anyone who you would suggest I talk to about this?

Sarah: I can't think of anyone.

Investigator: Have you spoken to anyone other than your boyfriend about this? Anyone at work other than Miguel?

Sarah: No.

Investigator: Is there anything else you think I should know?

Sarah: I can't think of anything.

Sample Interview with the Respondent

Investigator: Hi Mitchell, I'm Jackson from HR. I'm here to investigate a complaint that you may have violated our sexual harassment policy.

Mitchell: You've got to be kidding. Who complained? What did they say?

Investigator: I can imagine you have a lot of questions and concerns, but let's take this one step at a time. I need to ask you some questions but first I want to explain the investigative process to you. I'm here as a neutral party, I've made no conclusions yet as to what happened. My role is to be a fact finder. I'll be taking notes for you to review and sign. I'm going to keep this matter as confidential as possible, and I need your cooperation in this.

Mitchell: I sure won't tell anyone. But you haven't told me who complained.

Investigator: Who complained is actually confidential. But during the course of the investigation I will tell you what the allegations are and give you an opportunity to respond.

Mitchell: Okay.

Investigator: I also want you to know it's against company policy—and the law—to retaliate against someone for bringing a complaint of harassment. Even if I don't tell you who complained, you may very well guess. I want your assurance that you will do nothing to retaliate. Okay?

Mitchell: But what if it's all a lie?

Investigator: If someone intentionally brings a false complaint, they're subject to discipline. If there was a true misunderstanding, no one will be disciplined, and the complainant is protected from retaliation.

Mitchell: All right, let's get started, I want to know what this is about.

Investigator: Okay. Let me ask you some questions about your day yesterday. What time did you get to work?

Mitchell: I always get in at around eight.

Investigator: Is that when you came in yesterday?

Mitchell: Yes, about then, maybe a few minutes later.

Investigator: What did you do after you first got to work?

Mitchell: Turned on my computer, checked my e-mails.

Investigator: Was anyone else there?

Mitchell: It was pretty quiet; most people don't get in until about eight-thirty.

Investigator: Who was the first person you saw yesterday?

Mitchell: I don't know. Probably it was Sarah.

Investigator: Where was this?

Mitchell: Why? Was it Sarah who complained?

Investigator: I know it's hard not to know, but I really do need to ask you questions in a certain order. Where was Sarah when you first saw her yesterday?

Mitchell: In the break room.

Investigator: Was anyone else there?

Mitchell: I think Henry got in at about the same time. Once we're all in, someone usually makes coffee. Sarah made the coffee yesterday.

Investigator: Did anything unusual happen when she was making coffee?

Mitchell: No—what do you mean by that?

Investigator: The complaint we received is that you said something offensive to Sarah while she was making coffee. Did you say anything to her?

Mitchell: Nothing offensive. What did she say I said? I may've said good morning, but I didn't say anything else.

Investigator: Did you tell her that her body looked great?

Mitchell: No!

Investigator: Did you tell her you wanted to see what her body could do?

Mitchell: Of course not.

Investigator: There is an allegation that you came up behind Sarah and said her body looked great, you'd like to see what it can do. Did you say that to her?

Mitchell: No.

Investigator: Did you say anything like that to her or to anyone else?

Mitchell: No.

Investigator: Can you think of any reason someone would say you said this?

Mitchell: Maybe if someone didn't like me.

Investigator: Is there someone specific you're thinking about?

Mitchell: No.

Investigator: What was Sarah's manner when you saw her yesterday morning?

Mitchell: Normal.

Investigator: Did she seem upset or anything?

Mitchell: No, I didn't notice anything unusual.

Investigator: What kind of relationship do you have with Sarah?

Mitchell: What do you mean by that?

Investigator: Are you friendly at work, have you seen her outside of work?

Mitchell: We're just co-workers.

Investigator: Is there anyone who you would suggest I talk to about this?

Mitchell: I can't think of anyone.

Investigator: Is there anything else you think I should know?

Mitchell: I wouldn't do something like this.

Sample Interview with a Witness

Investigator: Hi Henry, I'm Jackson from HR. I'm here to investigate a complaint of a possible violation of our sexual harassment policy. It doesn't involve you, but you may have witnessed something. I need to ask you some questions but first I want to explain the investigative process to you. I'll be taking notes for you to review and sign. I'm going to keep this matter as confidential as possible and I need your cooperation in this.

Henry: I sure won't tell anyone.

Investigator: I also want you to know it's against company policy and the law to retaliate against someone for participating in the investigation of a complaint of harassment. If you experience anything you think is retaliation, let me know right away.

Henry: All right.

Investigator: Okay, let me ask you some questions about your day yesterday. What time did you get to work?

Henry: About eight-thirty.

Investigator: What did you do after you first got to work?

Henry: Turned on my computer, checked my e-mails.

Investigator: Was anyone else there?

Henry: It was pretty quiet. Mitchell and Sarah were already in the break room.

Investigator: How do you know that?

Henry: After I got to my desk I went to the break room and saw Mitchell and Sarah.

Investigator: Where were they standing?

Henry: Why? Was it Sarah who complained?

Investigator: I actually can't tell you that. Where were they standing?

Henry: Okay. Well, they were standing by the coffee maker.

Investigator: Did you hear them say anything?

Henry: No, Sarah turned and walked out just when I walked in.

Investigator: Did you notice anything before she walked out?

Henry: She left quickly, flustered, like maybe she was upset about something.

Investigator: Does Sarah often appear upset or flustered?

Henry: No.

Investigator: Have you ever seen her upset or flustered before?

Henry: No.

Investigator: What do you know about Mitchell and Sarah's relationship?

Henry: Not much. Nothing unusual.

Investigator: Have you ever heard either of them say or do anything you'd consider inappropriate at work?

Henry: No.

Investigator: Do you have the sense that either has a romantic interest in the other?

Henry: No.

Investigator: Is there anything else you think I should know?

Henry: I can't think of anything.

Sample Notes

Interview with Sarah

Usual admonitions given.

Told boyfriend and supervisor Miguel—no one else.

Mitchell "came on to me."

Yesterday—8:30—break room—S at coffee machine.

Just them—Henry came in.

Hasn't spoken to Henry. Told supervisor (Miguel).

S—M said she, "Had such a great body, wanted to see what it could do." Gave her creeps.

M walked up while making coffee. Stood behind her and said above.

Looked at him and walked out.

No previous behavior.

Knows no one else he made uncomfortable.

Doesn't know why did this.

Suggests no one else to talk to.

Interview with Mitchell

Usual admonitions given.

Came in 8 yesterday. Checked e-mails.

First person saw was S in break room. Henry may've been there too.

Denied allegations.

Said nothing to S. S didn't seem upset.

Can't think of why would make up.

No one can think of to talk to.

Interview with Henry

Usual admonitions given.

Arrived yesterday at 8:30. Checked e-mails. Mitchell and Sarah already in break room.

Went to break room—saw M & S standing by coffee maker. Heard nothing.

Sarah turned and walked out as he walked in—S seemed upset.

Hasn't seen S upset before.

Has no other info.

Sample Statements

Statement of Sarah Employee

Yesterday at about 8:30 a.m., while I was making coffee in the break room, my co-worker Mitchell said, "You have such a great body, I want to see what it can do." He said this in my right ear, while standing behind me. I did not respond and immediately walked out of the room. As I walked out, our co-worker, Henry walked in. I was offended by Mitchell's comment. This was the only time he has said something offensive to me and I know of no reason why he would do so. I told my boyfriend Steve and my supervisor what happened. I have not told anyone else.

Statement of Mitchell Co-worker

Yesterday shortly after I arrived at work I saw Sarah in the break room. Henry was in the break room at about the same time. Sarah was making coffee. I did not say anything to Sarah. I certainly did not tell her that her body looked great or that I wanted to see what her body could do or anything to that effect. She did not seem upset. I noticed nothing unusual.

Statement of Henry Jones

Yesterday after I arrived at work I went to the break room and saw Mitchell and Sarah standing by the coffee maker. I did not hear them say anything. Sarah turned and walked out just when I walked in. She seemed upset and flustered. I have not seen her upset or flustered before. I have never heard either Sarah or Mitchell say anything inappropriate at work and I know nothing about their relationship.

Sample Investigative Report

Here is a sample report using the investigation of Sarah's complaint against Mitchell. Some of the interview notes and statements for this investigation appear in Appendix E. This sample report is based on the premise that other witnesses have been spoken to and that further interviews were conducted with the complainant and respondent.

DATE: July XX, XXXX

TO: Executive Director

FROM: Investigator [Name]

SUBJECT: Report of Findings

Background

On July XX, XXXX, Sarah Employee contacted her supervisor, Miguel Lopez, regarding a complaint of possible sexual harassment. The allegation was made against her co-worker, Mitchell Co-worker. Ms. Employee alleged that on Tuesday June XX, XXXX, Mr. Co-Worker said in her right ear that she had a "great body" and he wanted to "see what it could do." Mr. Co-worker denied the behavior. The investigator spoke to five witnesses and concluded the investigation on July XX, XXXX.

Statement of Facts

Ms. Employee has worked at ABC as a Nursing Coordinator for six months. She was transferred here from XYZ Center, having worked there for twelve years, most recently as a Nursing Coordinator. Mitchell

Co-worker has worked in the same unit for two years. The only other employee in the unit is Henry Jones. Miguel Lopez, Program Director, supervises them.

On July XX, XXXX, Ms. Employee contacted her supervisor stating that she had been sexually harassed the day before. Ms. Employee was initially reluctant to state who had harassed her but ultimately stated that her co-worker, Mitchell Co-worker, approached her from behind just after she finished making coffee and said in her right ear that she had a "great body" and that he "wanted to see what it could do." Ms. Employee states this occurred at about 8:30 a.m. in the break room. She states she said nothing but left the room upset.

Ms. Employee states that their co-worker, Henry Jones, walked in as this occurred. She was unsure if he witnessed the incident. She did tell her boyfriend, Steve, about the incident, and also informed her supervisor, Miguel.

Mr. Co-worker denies making the statement attributed to him. According to Mr. Co-worker, he did see Sarah Employee that morning when she was making coffee, but he did not make any comment to her. He knows of no reason she would fabricate these allegations. He states he is unaware of her being upset that morning.

Henry Jones corroborated seeing Employee and Co-worker in the break room. He states that he heard nothing but that Employee left looking upset and flustered. Steve Ancel, Employee's boyfriend, corroborated the fact that Employee told him about the events of June XX. He states she was very upset. The investigator also spoke to Employee and Co-worker's supervisor, Miguel Lopez. Lopez states both are good employees and he is unaware of any relationship or tension between them.

An investigation of Ms. Employee's record and Mr. Co-worker's record at XYZ reveals nothing significant. Neither has made a prior complaint of harassment or been the subject of a harassment complaint.

Findings of Fact

It is always difficult to determine what occurred when the facts from the parties are diametrically opposed. Since Ms. Employee made a very specific allegation and Mr. Co-worker flatly denied it, it comes down to a credibility determination.

It is found that Ms. Employee was more credible than Mr. Co-worker for a number of reasons. First, there did not appear to be any motive for Ms. Employee to make up this story. Second, Ms. Employee discussed what occurred with her boyfriend, Steve Ancel, and with her supervisor. Third, while Mr. Jones did not hear Co-worker say anything, he did see Employee leave in a manner that he described as flustered. This corroborates that something happened that Employee found upsetting. Moreover, Co-worker denies that Employee was upset that day. Given the fact that Jones was aware of this, it is not credible that Co-worker was not. Rather, it indicates he is not providing the full story and undermines his credibility in denying the allegations.

Based on the above findings of fact, it is determined that there is sufficient evidence to find that Ms. Employee's allegations are true.

Recommendations

Note: Not all investigators are expected to make recommendations.

The allegations involve behavior in violation of ABC's rules. Thus, some disciplinary action should be taken. However, it is noted that there has been no prior discipline against Co-worker for anything similar. The conduct here was verbal, not physical, and was isolated. Under these circumstances it is recommended that Co-worker either be given a written warning or a brief suspension. It is also recommended that there be further training in the workgroup concerning sexual harassment and that the situation be monitored.

Sample Follow-up Letter

DATE: July XX, XXXX

TO: Sarah Employee

FROM: Executive Director

SUBJECT: Follow-up to Complaint of 7/X/XX

ABC's HR Director, Jackson West, recently completed an investigation of complaints that you made regarding potential violations of ABC's policy that prohibits harassment including sexual harassment. To begin, please accept my appreciation for bringing your complaint to our attention and for cooperating with the investigation. This memo will summarize the results of the investigation.

You complained about comments allegedly made by Mitchell Co-Worker in the break room on June XX, XXXX. Our investigation reached a finding that the behavior you alleged very likely occurred and that Mitchell Co-worker violated our company policy.

We have initiated appropriate disciplinary action as a result of the investigation's finding. Additionally, at an appropriate time in the near future, members of your workgroup, including supervisors and managers, will be participating in a harassment-free workplace training program.

As a reminder of the serious commitment our organization has to provide a work place for all employees that is free from harassment, I enclose a copy of the ABC policy. Please note the section of the policy that prohibits any form of retaliation for an employee, like you, who has participated in a complaint or an investigation of a complaint. If, at any time, you believe that you are being retaliated against for your action in bringing the complaints mentioned above, please do not hesitate to contact me via email or phone. If I am absent from the office, contact Jackson and let him know that you have an urgent need to speak with me about a private matter.

Thank you again for bringing your complaint forward and allowing us to apply our company policy.

APPENDIX H

Bibliography

Bernstein, Anita. Treating Sexual Harassment with Respect. *The Harvard Law Review*. 111 1997 445.

Blumenthal, Jeremy A. "A Wipe of the Hands, A Lick of the Lips: The Validity of Demeanor Evidence in Assessing Witness Credibility." *Nebraska Law Review*. 72 1993 1157.

Bravo, Ellen and Ellen Cassedy. *The 9 to 5 Guide to Combating Sexual Harassment: Candid Advice from 9 to 5, the National Association of Working Women*. (New York: John Wiley & Sons, Inc. 1992).

Covey, Anne. *The Workplace Law Advisor: From Harassment and Discrimination Policies to Hiring and Firing Guidelines—What Every Manager and Employee Needs to Know*. (Cambridge: Perseus Books Group 2000).

Deblieux, Mike and Dave Kirchner. *Stopping Sexual Harassment before It Starts: A Business and Legal Perspective*. (West Des Moines: American Media, Incorporated 1997).

EEOC Guidance on Vicarious Employer Liability for Unlawful Harassment by Supervisors. EEOC Notice Number 915.002, 6/18/99.

Fagan, Pamela, Jennifer R. George, Amy Nickell Jacobs, Laurie R. Jones and Susan Hance Sorrells. *Real Solutions: Strategies and Tools to Rid the Workplace of Harassment*. (Southlake: Employment Practices Solutions 1998).

Fitzgerald, Louise F., Fritz Drasgow, Charles L. Hulin, Michele J. Gelfand and Vicki J. Magley. "Antecedents and Consequences of Sexual Harassment in Organizations: A Test of an Integrated Model." *Journal of Applied Psychology*, 82 1997 4, 578-589.

Fitzgerald, Louise F., Michele J. Gelfand and Fritz Drasgow. "Measuring Sexual Harassment: Theoretical and Psychometric Advances." *Basic and Applied Social Psychology*, 17 1995 4, 425-445.

Fitzgerald, Louise F. and Suzanne Swan. "Why Didn't She Just Report Him? The Psychological and Legal Implications of Women's Responses to Sexual Harassment." *Journal of Social Issues*, 51 1995 1, 117-138.

Goleman, Daniel. *Emotional Intelligence.* (New York: Bantam 1995).

Gutek, Barbara A. *Sex and the Workplace.* (San Francisco: Jossey-Bass 1985).

Hemphill, Hellen and Ray Haines. *Discrimination, Harassment, and the Failure of Diversity Training.* (Westport: Quorum Books 1997).

Hill, Anita. *Speaking Truth to Power.* (New York: Anchor Books 1998)

Jensen, Inger W. and Barbara A. Gutek. "Attributions and Assignment of Responsibility in Sexual Harassment." *Journal of Social Issues*, 38 1992 4, 121-136.

Lindemann, Barbara and David D. Kadue. *Sexual Harassment in Employment Law.* (Washington, D.C.: The Bureau of National Affairs, Inc. 1992) (1997 supplement available).

MacKinnon, Catherine A. *Sexual Harassment of Working Women.* (New Haven and London: Yale University Press 1986).

Orlov, Darlene and Michael Roumell. *What Every Manager Needs to Know about Sexual Harassment.* (New York: AMACOM 1999).

Petrocelli, William and Barbara Kate Repa. *Sexual Harassment on the Job: What it is and how to stop it.* (Berkeley: Nolo Press 1998).

Sexual Harassment in the Federal Workplace: Is it a Problem? A report of the U.S. Merit Systems Protection Board, Office of Merit Systems Review and Studies, Washington, D.C. 1981.

Sexual Harassment in the Federal Government: An Update, A report to the President and the Congress of the United States by the U.S. Merit Systems Protection Board, Washington, D.C. 1988.

Sexual Harassment in the Federal Workplace: Trends, Progress, Continuing Challenges, A report to the President and the Congress of the United States by the U.S. Merit Systems Protection Board, Washington, D.C., 1995.

Sexual Harassment Survey, Society for Human Resources Management. SHRM Foundation, 1999.

Sumrall, Amber Coverdale and Dena Taylor, editors. *Sexual Harassment: Women Speak Out.* (Freedom, CA: The Crossing Press 1992).

Tannen, Deborah. *Talking From 9 to 5, Women and Men in the Workplace: Language, Sex and Power* (New York: Avon Books 1995).

Weiss, Donald. *Fair, Square & Legal: Safe Hiring, Managing, & Firing Practices to Keep You & Your Company Out of Court.* (New York: AMACOM 1999).

Index

About the Authors

Amy Oppenheimer, J.D., an attorney for over 20 years, is a recognized expert in the field of preventing and responding to workplace harassment. She obtained her J.D. from University of California, Davis in 1980. She then litigated cases of workplace harassment for 12 years before becoming a neutral in the field.

Since 1992, Oppenheimer has acted as a neutral in employment law in a number of capacities. She is an administrative law judge for the California Unemployment Appeals Board. She is on the American Arbitration Association's panel of employment mediators and arbitrators. As a senior consultant, she has trained *Fortune* 500 and smaller employers in preventing harassment. She has acted as a neutral investigator, testified in court as an expert, and spoken and written widely on the topic of harassment.

Oppenheimer is a member of the Association for Conflict Resolution and of the State Bar of California. She is a former President of the Board of Directors of Berkeley Dispute Resolution Services, a nonprofit organization providing mediation services to the community.

Craig Pratt, SPHR, MSW, is principal owner of a consulting firm providing expertise in human resources management.

Pratt consults for corporations, public agencies, and law firms in applying the principles of human resource management to investigating harassment and discrimination. He has conducted high profile, large-scale investigations into harassment. He trains investigators and evaluates investigations as an expert in court. From 1990–2000, he was a retained expert in more than 350 court cases, including the landmark case Ellison v. Brady.

He has consulted to the U.S. Equal Employment Opportunity Commission and the California Department of Fair Employment and Housing. He has testified before the California Senate and Assembly regarding harassment investigations.

Pratt has been an HR practitioner and manager for the Standard Oil Company and Hallmark Cards. He is certified as a Senior Professional in Human Resources (SPHR) and serves on the Board of Governors of the Consultants Forum of the Society for Human Resource Management. His Master's in Social Work (MSW) is from the University of California at Berkeley.

Selected Titles from the Society for Human Resource Management (SHRM)

■ *Human Resource Essentials: Your Guide to Starting and Running the HR Function*
By Lin Grensing-Pophal, SPHR

■ *Legal, Effective References: How to Give and Get Them*
By Wendy Bliss, J.D., SPHR

■ *Solutions for Human Resource Managers*
By the SHRM Information Center Staff

■ *Supervisor's Guide to Labor Relations*
By T.O. Collier, Jr.

TO ORDER SHRM BOOKS

SHRM offers a member discount on all books that it publishes or sells. To order this or any other book published by the Society, contact the SHRMStore.™

ONLINE: www.shrm.org/shrmstore

BY PHONE: 800-444-5006 (option #1); or 770-442-8633 (ext. 362); or TDD 703-548-6999

BY FAX: 770-442-9742

BY MAIL: SHRM Distribution Center
             P.O. Box 930132
             Atlanta, GA 31193-0132
             USA